Windows® Phone 7 Plain & Simple

Michael Stroh

Published with the authorization of Microsoft Corporation by:
O'Reilly Media, Inc.
1005 Gravenstein Highway North
Sebastopol, California 95472

Printed and bound in the United States of America.

1 2 3 4 5 6 7 8 9   QG   5 4 3 2 1 0

Microsoft Press titles may be purchased for educational, business or sales promotional use. Online editions are also available for most titles (*http://my.safaribooksonline.com*). For more information, contact our corporate/institutional sales department: (800) 998-9938 or *corporate@ oreilly.com*. Visit our website at *microsoftpress.oreilly.com*. Send comments to *mspinput@microsoft.com*.

Acquisitions and Developmental Editors: Rosemary Caperton and Kenyon Brown
Production Editor: Rachel Monaghan
Copy Editor: John Pierce
Proofreader: Nancy Sixsmith
Technical Reviewer: Michael Stroh
Indexer: Potomac Indexing, LLC
Compositors: Ron Bilodeau and Nellie McKesson
Cover: Karen Montgomery
Illustrator: Robert Romano

978-0-735-64342-0

Contents

4   Typing and Using Speech   43

5   Talking on the Phone   57

14 ## Shopping for Apps and Playing Games **201**

15 ## Working with Office Mobile **221**

What do you think of this book? We want to hear from you!

Microsoft is interested in hearing your feedback so we can continually improve our books and learning resources for you. To participate in a brief online survey, please visit:

www.microsoft.com/learning/booksurvey/

Acknowledgments

Many people at Microsoft were generous with their time and expertise despite the daily pressures of trying to create a smartphone that would surprise the world. A big thank you to my colleagues on the Windows Phone consumer content team: Deborah Baumfeld, Teresa Goertz, Rachel Herbert, Erica Kerwien, Andy Myers, Mandy Oei, Elizabeth Reese, and John Shaw. I'm especially grateful to Matt Lichtenberg, for cheerfully offering to review several early chapters and spotting some embarrassing blunders, and to Karen Kesler for her rock-steady support from start to finish and making Studio F a more fun place to work.

On the gutsy and whip-smart Windows Phone engineering team, thanks to Doug Adams, Itai Almog, Scott Borton, Andrew Duke, Rich Grutzmacher, Thomas Kuehnel, KC Lemson, Steve May, Li-Juan Qin, Yili Aiwazian Wang, Kerry Woolsey, and many others. Rosemary Caperton and Ben Ryan at Microsoft Press helped shape and shepherd the initial idea for this book, while Sumita Mukherji, Rachel Monaghan, John Pierce, and Ken Brown at O'Reilly Media made it a physical reality. Any errors that remain are entirely my own.

Nothing would be possible without Maya, Yoshi, and most of all Kunise, who provided the humor, back pats, and occasional butt kicks I needed to get the job done, while doing more than her fair share of parenting along the way. I owe you more than I can ever repay.

Finally, I'd like to dedicate this book to my parents, Jack and Sue, for sparking a lifelong love of books and curiosity about how things work. We miss you, Mom.

—Michael Stroh

1 About This Book

Congratulations! You now own one of the most original and fun new phones to emerge on the scene in years. (But you knew that already, didn't you?) Windows Phone 7 represents an exciting new direction for both Microsoft and the evolution of the smartphone, those magical do-everything devices that are part phone, part pocket computer.

Since Microsoft provided the first public sneak-peeks of Windows Phone 7 in early 2010, it has generated an enormous amount of excitement and buzz. Microsoft designers threw away the industry cookbook and set out to completely rethink how a great smartphone operating system should look and behave. The result is what you see in your hands and on the pages of this book—a phone that's radically different not only from competitors like Apple and Google but even from Microsoft's own previous effort, Windows Mobile.

Windows Phone 7 can claim several firsts. It's the first phone to combine so many of Microsoft's most popular and useful products, from Bing and Internet Explorer to Office and Xbox LIVE. The phone also introduces *Live tiles* and *hubs*, two ingenious time-saving ways to display and organize information. But as good as this smartphone operating system is, Microsoft has made it clear that it's just getting warmed up.

As I write this, on the cusp of the much-anticipated public launch of Windows Phone 7, you can bet that Windows Phone engineers are already busily dreaming up ways to make their creation even more fun, more useful, and more indispensible for everyday life.

No Computerspeak!

If you want to get the most from Windows Phone 7 in the shortest amount of time and the least amount of effort—and who wouldn't?—this is the book for you. Some people enjoy noodling around for hours trying to understand how technology works. *Windows Phone 7 Plain & Simple* is for the rest of us. It will help you have fun and do more with your new Windows Phone from Day 1, while spending as little time as possible with your nose against the page (or screen, for the e-book crowd).

Like the rest of the Plain & Simple series, this book is written in plain English—no technobabble or computerspeak allowed! And it's organized around tasks: discrete step-by-step recipes for doing something useful on your phone—making a conference call, playing a song, sending an e-mail. To get started, simply find the tasks that interest you and follow the steps. No single task in any Plain & Simple book spans more than two pages. But they all come with annotated, full-color photos to make the steps easier to follow.

There's another handy Plain & Simple convention you should watch for. Occasionally you'll see one or more colored boxes on the page. The *See Also* box highlights related tasks worth checking out, while *Tips* offers shortcuts and extra information about a task. *Try This* provides ideas for using Windows Phone 7, and a *Caution* warns you of potential problems or obstacles you might encounter.

But ultimately, tasks (with pretty pictures) are the heart and soul of this book, as well as the philosophy that the information you care about should be available at a glance and be *plain and simple*.

A Quick Overview

You don't have to read this book from front to back (in fact, I'm betting you probably won't). But if this is your first smartphone, you might find it useful to start your exploration with Sections 2 and 3, which walk you through the new Windows Phone 7 interface and show you how to quickly set up and personalize your phone. But again, it's totally your call.

Here's what you'll find on these pages:

Section 2 takes you on a guided tour of Windows Phone 7, from its modern interface to the buttons and navigational gestures that help you get around. You'll learn about some of the status indicators you'll see and the transmitters, sensors, and other electronics that make your phone work.

Section 3 covers all the setup and housekeeping tasks you'll probably want to do on your new phone in the first few hours and days—things like setting up e-mail or Facebook accounts, choosing ringtones and color schemes, and connecting to Wi-Fi networks or a hands-free Bluetooth headset.

Section 4 focuses on the on-screen keyboard and speech recognition features in Windows Phone 7, two important ways to enter information and commands. You'll learn tricks for typing faster on the touch-screen and how to use speech recognition to make calls, surf the Web, and more.

Section 5 is all about the phone part of Windows Phone 7. Making calls is presumably why you bought a phone in the first place. So this section covers basic dialing, checking your voice-mail, using in-call features such as speakerphone and hold, and advanced features such as conference calls and call forwarding.

Section 6 explains the People hub, the place to connect with your friends and other contacts. In this section, you'll learn how to create and maintain a contacts list and how to browse your Facebook feed and post responses.

Section 7 focuses on e-mail. You learn how to check and send e-mail on your phone, how to open and save attachments, manage your mailbox folders, and sort and search through your messages for a specific one.

Section 8 covers texting. It shows you how to read, compose, send, forward, and reply to text messages. You'll also learn how to include pictures in a text message.

Section 9 focuses on the Calendar app. You'll learn how to create and edit appointments, send and answer invitations, juggle multiple calendars, and toggle between month, day, and agenda views.

Section 10 is all about browsing the Web with Internet Explorer Mobile. I'll cover how to open a web page and take advantage of tabs for viewing multiple pages. You'll learn how to search the Web on your phone and save favorite sites, and discover what the Mobile Web is all about.

Section 11 covers the Maps app, which helps you figure out where you are and the location of a place you want to visit. You'll learn how to get turn-by-turn directions, check traffic conditions, and browse customer reviews of stores and restaurants to find good places to shop and eat.

Section 12 shows you how to entertain yourself with the Music + Videos hub. You'll learn how to play music, videos, and podcasts on your phone and how to tune in FM radio stations.

Section 13 focuses on taking and enjoying pictures with the Pictures hub and camera. You'll learn how to take pictures and record videos, upload your pictures to the Web, and save pictures to your phone. You'll also find out how you can personalize the Pictures hub with your own snapshots.

Section 14 is one of those parts of the book that you'll probably find yourself wanting to dive in and read early. It's about getting apps and games for your phone from Marketplace. It also explains how to buy music and videos and what the Games hub featuring Xbox LIVE is all about.

Section 15 is all business—literally. It covers the Office hub, home to Office Mobile and its associated apps: Word, Excel, PowerPoint, OneNote, and SharePoint Workspace.

Finally, Section 16 is another must-read because it covers synching your phone to your PC using the companion Zune software. A free download, the Zune software makes it easy to back up pictures and videos you've taken on your phone, and stock your phone with music and videos from your PC's multimedia library.

A Few Assumptions

You were an important part of the planning of this book. As I sat down to write, I wondered: What do you most want to know about your new Windows Phone? Have you owned a smartphone before? How comfortable are you with computers and technology? I'm guessing that for many of you, this is your first smartphone. (Trust me: You're in for a treat.) So I'm not expecting you to have any specific background knowledge—other than perhaps that you've made a phone call at some point in your life.

The book assumes your phone has a cellular data plan through your carrier. Without an Internet connection, many of the phone's most fun and useful features—browsing and searching the Web, getting turn-by-turn directions—won't work.

Finally, don't be surprised if your phone—and especially its Start screen—looks a bit different from what I show in the book. That's okay. In fact, it's inevitable. Microsoft went to great lengths to make sure that all Windows Phones look and behave the same, no matter which electronics company makes the actual handset or which carrier provides service.

But your phone might have a few preinstalled apps that mine doesn't. The Start screen might also be a different color or have the tiles arranged in a different order. Windows Phone 7 is *so* much fun to decorate and personalize that few phones (like mine) remain in the default factory configuration for long. None of that should hinder you from following the tasks in this book.

A Final Word (or Two)

My hope is that every page of *Windows Phone 7 Plain & Simple* offers at least one surprise—a feature you didn't know existed, a tip you haven't read elsewhere.

Who am I to make such promises? Well, I've spent the last year working alongside the crack team of Microsoft designers and engineers that created the new operating system. I sat in on their meetings, cornered them in their offices, and peppered them with questions by the coffee machine. I've also spent many hours playing with and testing Windows Phone 7 in the months prior to its official launch. Along the way, I jotted down every trick, every shortcut, every secret about it I could find. This book is the result.

One of the fun things about technology is that it's always changing, always evolving. But that also makes life a nightmare for how-to writers! It's unclear what additions or updates Microsoft has planned in the months ahead for its new phone software. But a good place to keep up with breaking news and changes is the Windows Phone website, and especially its How-to section (which I also work on, by the way). You can find it at *www.windowsphone.com*.

I hope you find this book useful—and that you have as much fun with your Windows Phone as I do with mine. If you have any questions, suggestions, or spot any errors, I'd love to hear from you. Drop me a line sometime at *wp7rocks@live.com*.

Taking a Quick Tour

Smartphones are the Swiss Army knives of the twenty-first century. And Windows Phone 7 is no exception. It's a camera, a media player, a game console, a web browser, a GPS navigator, an alarm clock, a scientific calculator—oh, did I mention it also makes calls? And that's just for starters. It's also a pocket computer capable of running whatever creative new software applications—or *apps*—the legions of programmers out there dream up in the months and years ahead.

Windows Phone 7 is also something of a greatest-hits package—the first Microsoft offering to weave together so many of the company's popular products and services. As you look around your phone, you'll see elements of Bing, Internet Explorer, Office, Windows Live, Xbox, and Zune. As a result, parts of your new phone will probably feel instantly familiar.

Or not. The other thing Windows Phone 7 has going for it is that it's not just another iPhone clone. (I'm talking to you, Android.) Microsoft has made a big deal about Windows Phone 7 being "a different kind of phone." You can't always trust marketing hype, of course, but in this case Microsoft is right: From its modern looks to its novel approach to organizing and delivering information, there's no other phone quite like Windows Phone 7. So before we go any farther, let's take a quick tour and see what the fuss is about.

Starting with Start

On a PC, you'd call it the desktop. On other smartphones, it's the home screen. But when you power up Windows Phone 7 for the first time, the place you find yourself after setting up is *Start*.

The Start screen is many things: It's a launch pad for apps; a source of news and information; a gallery of shortcuts to favorite contacts, pictures, and other important things. Start is the center of the Windows Phone 7 universe, so important there's even a dedicated button on your phone (the *Start* button, naturally) to instantly whisk you there from anywhere on the phone.

Notice how lively the Start screen looks compared to other phones. In place of static rows of icons, you'll see stacked colored blocks. Microsoft calls them *Live tiles*. Think of them like tiny animated billboards. Some flash your tally of missed calls and messages, or the details of upcoming appointments. Others are purely for entertainment. The Games tile, for instance, shows your bobbing Xbox avatar. The Pictures tile displays a favorite photo, while the faces of your contacts pop up on People.

Live tiles are constantly updated and show info like missed calls or texts and upcoming appointments

Flick up or down to see more tiles

Tap for the Apps list

Tap a tile to open an app or hub

Games and Pictures are two of the six *hubs*, a new way to organize and browse info

Personalize Your Phone

Microsoft made the Start screen easy to personalize. You can push tiles around with your finger, pin new tiles to Start, or decorate them different colors. Windows Phone has two background themes—light and dark—and 10 different accent colors to choose from. If you grow tired of a tile, it's easy to remove it.

See All Your Apps

The Start screen has a hidden side. Swipe left on the screen, or tap the arrow on the top right, and you'll see the *Apps list*, an A-to-Z catalog of the programs installed on your phone—or, I should say, most of the programs. There's one important exception: games. Any game you install shows up only in the Games hub. For anything else, look here.

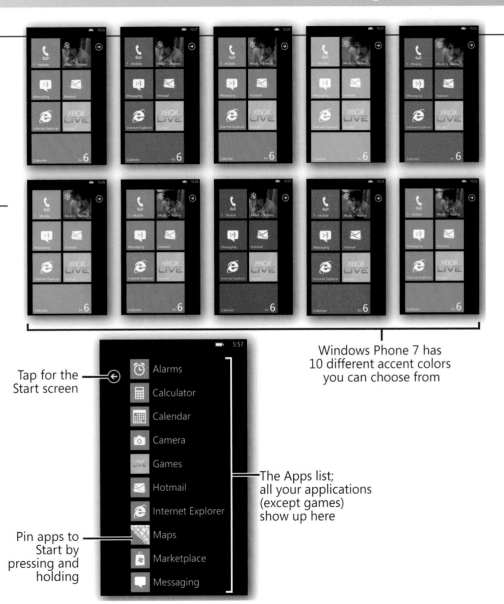

Windows Phone 7 has 10 different accent colors you can choose from

Tap for the Start screen

The Apps list; all your applications (except games) show up here

Pin apps to Start by pressing and holding

Alarms
Calculator
Calendar
Camera
Games
Hotmail
Internet Explorer
Maps
Marketplace
Messaging

Saying Hello to Hubs

All smartphone makers today face the same essential quandary: How do you cram enough information on a phone's tiny screen? Live tiles are one creative solution. But Microsoft designers didn't stop there. In Windows Phone 7, they introduced a new organizational concept called *hubs*.

Hubs are horizontal panoramas of related information. Only a slice of the hub is visible at any one moment, but it's easy to see the rest—simply swipe your finger left or right on the screen to pan across.

Hubs make it easier to show lots of useful info without resorting to tapping open multiple apps. The People hub, for example, packages together an address book, a list of recent contacts, and an up-to-date feed from Facebook and Windows Live—all within three quick flicks of each other. People is one of six hubs on the phone. The others are:

- Pictures
- Music + Videos
- Games
- Office
- Marketplace

The Marketplace hub is one of six hubs in Windows Phone 7

The Lock Screen

The *lock screen* appears automatically if you don't touch your phone's screen for a short period (the default is one minute, but you can easily change it). Its main purpose is to protect you from doing something embarrassing, like pocket-dialing someone as you walk down the street. Think of it like a cover sheet for your phone. When the lock screen is visible, your touch-sensitive screen no longer responds to random poking. Getting past the lock screen requires you to swipe your finger. If you turn on your phone's password-protection feature, you have to swipe and then tap in your secret four-digit code.

But the lock screen is helpful in other ways, too. It shows the time and date; your next calendar appointment; the number of missed calls, e-mails, or texts; and whether you've set an alarm. It's also designed for fun. For example, turn it into a portable picture frame by replacing the background image, or *wallpaper*, with a photo from your on-camera collection.

Alarm set

Time, day, and date

Next appointment or event

The status bar and notification area

Swipe your finger upward to see the Start screen

Missed calls, texts, or emails

Pushing Buttons

Every Windows Phone 7, no matter which company makes it, comes with a basic set of buttons designed to save time and make life easier.

Back

As you hop around from app to app and hub to hub, Windows Phone keeps track of your travels. The Back button helps you retrace your steps (think of the Back button on a web browser). Pressing Back returns you to whatever you were looking at last, eventually taking you all the way back to Start.

Back also serves as a means to cancel or escape. Press it to exit a menu or cancel out of a dialog box.

Start

The Start button does two things. Tapping it (as you might expect) immediately transports you back to the Start screen, no matter where you are or what you're doing on the phone. Pressing and holding the button for a few moments activates the phone's speech recognition feature, which you can learn more about in "Talking to Your Phone" on page 54.

Search

The Search button make it easier to find stuff on or off your phone. As you'll quickly discover, the button is context-sensitive: What it looks for depends on what you're doing when you press it.

To find	Press the Search button from
Something on the Web	Start, Internet Explorer (see page 142)
An e-mail	An e-mail account (see page 95)
A place or address	Maps (see page 158)
A contact	People (see page 76)
A new app	Marketplace (see page 205)
A call	Call History (see page 60)

Camera

It's not one of the Big Three, but the Camera button is special nonetheless, and it does something that sets it apart from other smartphones out there: It lets you take a picture fast, even if the phone is asleep or locked. Just hold the button down and count to three. Boom—you're ready to snap away.

Volume

By making the phone's built-in speaker louder or softer, the volume buttons do what you probably expect. But they also do something you probably don't: Expose a hidden audio menu. The volume bar shows the current loudness and ringer settings. You can tap the Ring icon to toggle between vibrate and silent modes. If you're playing music or listening to a podcast, you'll also see a set of basic playback controls.

Camera

Back   Start   Search

Mini-playback control

Volume bar ——   —— Ring/vibrate toggle

Understanding Status and Notifications

Windows Phone 7 has a status bar at the top of the screen that provides at-a-glance info about the health and well-being of your phone—whether you have a signal, how strong it is, what network you're connected to, how long before your battery goes kaput. It's also where you'll see notifications—pop-up messages that preview the first line of an incoming text message or remind you who's on hold.

Notifications show you who just texted or who's on hold

Status Symbols

The Windows Phone 7 status bar has a few interesting quirks. In their quest to keep the screen clutter free, Microsoft engineers made the status bar hide itself after a few moments. If you need to see it, swipe down with your finger. Here are some of the more common icons you'll encounter and what they mean.

Icon	What it means
	Battery level
	Battery charging
	Cellular signal strength
	No cell signal
	Roaming
	Vibrate mode
	Silent mode
	Bluetooth
	Wi-Fi signal
	Airplane mode
	Call forwarding
	Locked SIM card
	No SIM card

The ABCs of Cellular Networks

Glance up at the status bar, right next to the familiar cell signal-strength indicator, and you'll probably see one or more letters. This code indicates the type of cellular data network you're connected to. Put simply, it's your Internet connection, and the code tells you something about how speedy it is (or isn't).

The fun of having a Windows Phone really becomes obvious when you're connected to the Internet. Only then can you surf the Web, send and receive e-mail, map an address with Bing, update Facebook, or download music and apps.

While Wi-Fi is always an option for connecting (see "Connecting to a Wi-Fi Hotspot" on page 22), most of the time your Internet link comes via your carrier's cellular data network. As of this writing, Windows Phone 7 is compatible only with carriers that use a *GSM network*, such as AT&T and T-Mobile. Sometime in 2011, Microsoft says it expects to have a version of Windows Phone 7 available for *CDMA networks*, the type used by Verizon and Sprint. Here's a brief rundown of the codes you're likely to encounter as you cruise around with your phone.

Letter	Data network	How fast it is
G	GPRS	The granddaddy of cellular data networks and also the slowest.
E	EDGE	Faster than GPRS—but not by much.
3G	UMTS	Now we're talking. 3G, or "third-generation," networks make web surfing and other data-intensive tasks bearable. But 3G coverage around the country is still spotty.
H	HSDPA	If you see an H, give a silent cheer. HSDPA is 3G on steroids.

Caution

Microsoft lets carriers customize the symbols that represent each type of data network. While the ones listed here are standard, what you see on your Windows Phone might not always correspond to this list.

Exploring Inside Your Phone

I often talk about Windows Phone 7 as though it's the entire phone, but it's actually just the name of Microsoft's software *operating system* that makes the phone work. Other companies build the device itself. As a result, the phone in your pocket might look very different from the Windows Phone in mine. Yours might have a slide-out keyboard, a curvier shape, or more buttons.

But inside it's a different story. Microsoft wanted every one of its phones—no matter who makes it or sells it—to have the same minimum list of features. (Notice I said *minimum*. If your phone comes with a bigger screen or better camera than the ones I list below—well, lucky you!)

So let's pull the covers off your new phone and take a quick peek at its silicon guts—if only because this is what makes a smartphone so darn much fun!

The Camera

Every Windows Phone comes with a 5-megapixel camera. Five megapixels is pretty darn good for a cell phone camera (8 megapixels is about the max on any phone these days) and more than up to the task of taking great snapshots and videos. Windows Phones can also record 720p-resolution high-definition video.

The Screen

Your phone comes with a 480×800-pixel color screen that's sensitive to human touch. In fact, the screen on your phone (a capacitance screen, if you must know) *only* responds to human touch—not a stylus, pencil tip, or finger nail. (Don't believe me? Try it.) It also knows when you're touching with two fingers. Some apps, like Maps, Internet Explorer, and Outlook, are designed to take advantage of this. (See "Navigating with Your Fingers" on page 15.)

The Radios

Every Windows Phone can send and receive various kinds of wireless signals—collectively these transmitters and receivers are known as the phone's *radios*. The biggie, of course, is the cellular radio responsible for voice and Internet data. But there's also a GPS radio for getting a fix on your location, a Bluetooth radio for hands-free headsets and headphones, and a Wi-Fi radio for connecting to Internet "hotspots" at home or in your favorite coffee shop. As a bonus, there's also an FM radio, something you don't find in many phones.

The Sensors

Sensors are the secret weapon of any smartphone. Every Windows Phone has at least four sensors on board. There's a light sensor to automatically brighten or dim the screen, making it easier to see during the day and help conserve battery power at night.

There's an accelerometer for sensing motion and orientation, a digital compass (aka the *magnetometer*), and a proximity sensor that automatically switches off the touch-sensitive screen when you have the phone pressed to your face.

Navigating with Your Fingers

If you're arriving from the PC world of point and click, you're in for a fun surprise. Windows Phone is operated using a series of finger gestures. If you're new to touch-screen smartphones, it might take you a few minutes to get the gist of gestures, but you'll quickly master them. And don't be surprised if you find yourself starting to touch every screen you encounter from now on, expecting a response.

Tap

The smartphone equivalent of a mouse click, tapping is the basic way to get stuff done on your phone and the first maneuver you need to master. You tap to launch apps, open web links, type text with the on-screen keyboard, and respond to pop-up notifications on your phone. Occasionally you double-tap the screen to do something—for example, zoom in or out on a picture or web page.

Press and Hold

Like many smartphones, Windows Phone 7 is loaded with hidden menus. Pressing and holding your finger against the screen for a few moments is the key to revealing them—and accessing many of the phone's coolest features. If you remember just one thing from this section, it should be this: When you get stuck or confused, try press and hold. It's your secret weapon.

Flick and Swipe

Flicking is a fast swipe of your finger in any direction across the screen. Flicking is ideal for quickly scrolling up and down a contact list or web page. The move is also handy in hubs, which you get around by using a flick left or right.

A word of caution: You'll quickly discover that there's some real-world physics at play in Windows Phone. Flick too quickly, and you might see the app, contact, or whatever you wanted to find whiz by in a blur. Sometimes a controlled swipe is more called for—for example, to slide open the lock screen or toggle a setting switch on or off.

Pinch and Spread

A two-fingered maneuver. These gestures are handy in apps like Internet Explorer, Maps, Pictures, and Mail—all places where you might need to zoom in or out to get a better look at something. They're easier to do than describe. Pinch your thumb and forefinger on the screen to make text or images smaller (zoom out). Spread them apart to do the opposite and zoom in.

3

Setting Up and Personalizing Your Windows Phone

You've just turned on Windows Phone for the first time, and the questions are no doubt already starting to pile up in your head. What's this? How can I do that? If this is your first smartphone, you might even feel a little overwhelmed.

It's okay.

Although Windows Phone is really a PC in disguise, I assure you it's a lot more fun—and easier to master—than the one on your desk. The goal of this section is to get you set up with as little fuss as possible. By the time you finish, you'll be using your e-mail and Facebook accounts, know how to pick a ringtone that doesn't drive you crazy, and be able to decorate your phone with pictures of your boyfriend, wife, kids, pet turtle—or whatever else makes you happy.

A final piece of advice: The first time you turn on your phone, you're asked to register a Windows Live ID. If you use Microsoft services like Hotmail or Xbox LIVE, you already have a Live ID. Otherwise, you can create one. Your phone works perfectly fine without a Live ID, but you'll need one eventually to download apps and games from Marketplace, so I suggest signing up.

Setting Up E-Mail and Your Calendar

After tapping around and exploring your new phone a bit, you're probably eager to start actually doing stuff. Top of the list for most folks is setting up their e-mail, calendar, and contacts list. If you use one of the popular web-based services from Microsoft, Google, or Yahoo, adding it to your phone is a breeze: Just type your sign-in credentials, and Windows Phone does the rest. Ditto for your work accounts. If your company uses Microsoft Exchange Server 2007 or later (and many do), Windows Phone can do most of the account set up on your behalf.

Set Up Your Accounts

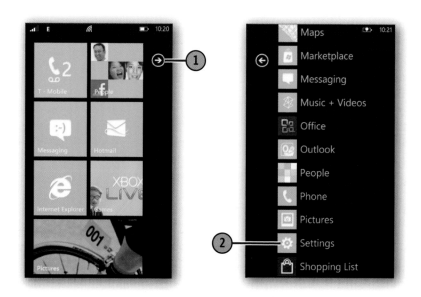

(1) On the Start screen, flick left to the Apps list or tap the arrow.

(2) Tap Settings.

(3) Tap Email & Accounts.

(4) Tap Add An Account.

(5) Do one of the following:

  • To set up a Yahoo, Windows Live, or Google account, tap its name.

  • To set up a Microsoft Exchange account for your work e-mail or calendar, tap Outlook.

  • To set up an ISP account that isn't listed (for example, AT&T, Comcast, or EarthLink), tap Other Account.

(6) Enter your e-mail address and password by tapping the appropriate box.

(7) When you're done, tap Sign In. Windows Phone attempts to find your account information and download any e-mail, contacts, and calendar entries.

Tip If you're setting up multiple accounts from the same provider—for example, two Gmail mailboxes—you can give each a unique name. Tap Settings > Email & Accounts. Tap the account, and then tap Account Name and type a new name.

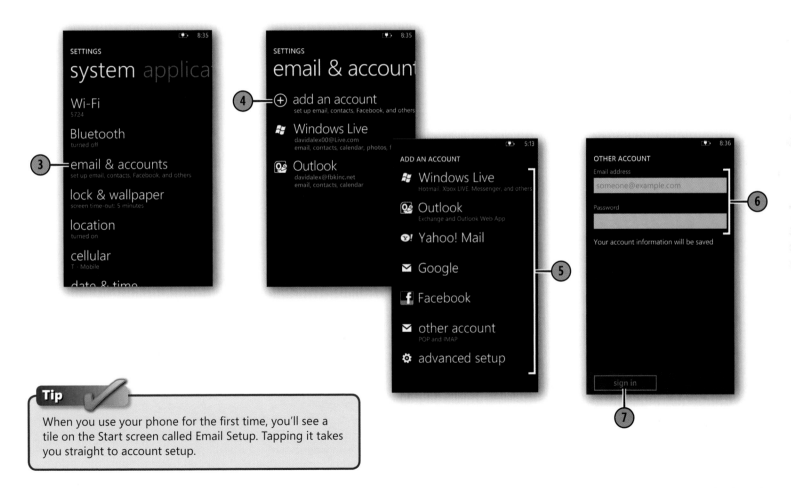

Tip

When you use your phone for the first time, you'll see a tile on the Start screen called Email Setup. Tapping it takes you straight to account setup.

Setting Up Facebook

If you're on Facebook—and with more than 500 million sub-scribers, who isn't nowadays?—you'll appreciate how Facebook-friendly Windows Phone 7 is. Once you set up your account, you can post pictures and messages and see and "like" other people's posts and pictures. Most of the Facebook action is found in three places on your phone: the People hub, the Pictures hub, and the Me card. If these aren't familiar yet, check out Section 6, "Connecting with People" (starting on page 73), and Section 13, "Taking Pictures and Videos" (starting on page 185).

Set Up Facebook

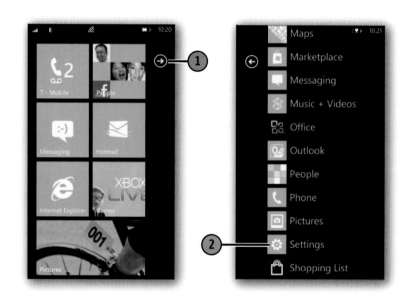

1. On the Start screen, flick left to the Apps list or tap the arrow.

2. Tap Settings.

3. Tap Email & Accounts.

4. Tap Add An Account.

5. Tap Facebook.

6. Type the e-mail address and pass-word you use to log on to your Face-book account.

7. Tap Sign In.

See Also

To learn more about seeing the pictures your friends have posted to Facebook, see "Viewing Pictures and Videos" on page 188. See "Posting to Facebook or Windows Live" on page 86 and "Working with the Me card" on page 88 to learn more about posting to Facebook or seeing what your friends have posted.

Tip

You can have only one Facebook account set up on your phone at a time. To add a different account, delete the existing one on your phone first.

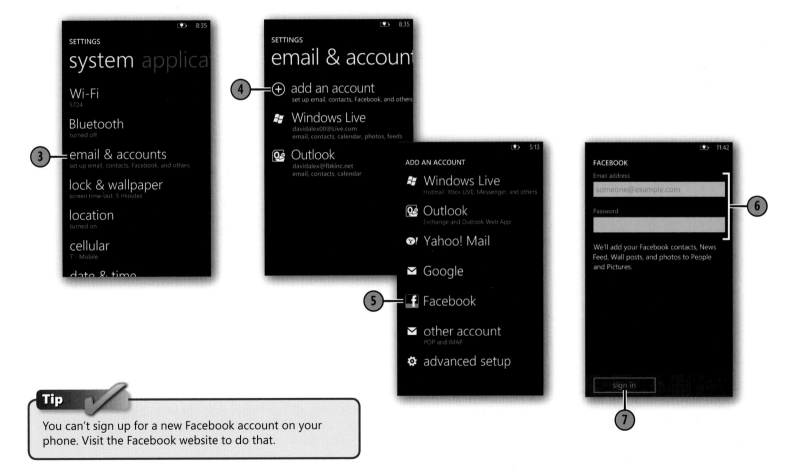

Tip

You can't sign up for a new Facebook account on your phone. Visit the Facebook website to do that.

Connecting to a Wi-Fi Hotspot

The fun of having a Windows Phone really becomes obvious only when you connect to the Internet. There are two ways to get it: a carrier's cellular data network or a Wi-Fi hotspot in a home, hotel, or coffee shop. You're probably already paying your carrier for the former, so why bother with Wi-Fi? One reason is speed. Wi-Fi is much faster than the typical cellular network. Once you're connected, look for the Wi-Fi icon on the phone's status bar. Windows Phone also remembers Wi-Fi networks you join and connects you automatically the next time you're in range.

Connect to Wi-Fi

1. If your phone detects a Wi-Fi hotspot in your vicinity, you'll see a notification. Tap it to connect. Otherwise, on the Start screen, flick left to the Apps list.

2. Tap Settings.

3. Under System, tap Wi-Fi.

4. Wi-Fi is turned on by default. If it's not turned on, tap the slider.

5. Tap the network you want to connect to.

6. If the connection is a secure network, you have to enter a password. (To make this easier, tap Show Password.)

7. Tap Done.

Caution

As of this writing, Windows Phone 7 can't connect to "hidden" Wi-Fi networks that don't broadcast their network name, or SSID. If you've hidden your network for security reasons, you need to unhide it to connect your phone.

Tip
Windows Phone 7 currently supports only 802.11b and 802.11g Wi-Fi networks, not the newer (and faster) 802.11n variety. But this shouldn't prevent you from connecting to most hotspots.

Tip
To disconnect from a Wi-Fi hotspot, press and hold the network name, and then tap Delete on the menu.

Customizing the Start Screen

If you don't like the arrangement of Live tiles on the Start screen, it's easy to redecorate. The tiles are all swappable, so you can stack them in whatever way makes the most sense to you. You can also pin favorite apps, contacts, or websites to Start so that they're always just a tap away. (A couple of obvious candidates for promotion to the Start screen are the Office and Maps apps, which are hidden away on the Apps list.)

If you want to pin a	See this page
Website	147
Contact	85
Map	168
Favorite picture	196
Game	215

Rearrange the Tiles

1. On the Start screen, press and hold a tile until it begins to float.

2. Drag the tile to a new spot with your finger, and then tap the tile to complete the move.

3. To remove a tile from Start, tap Unpin.

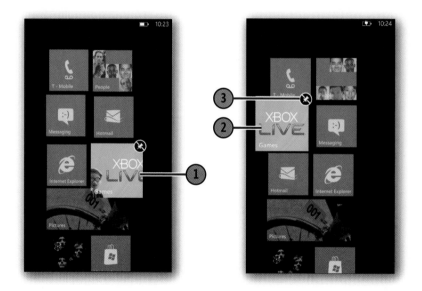

Pin an App to Start

1 On the Start screen, flick left to the Apps list or tap the arrow.

2 Press and hold the app you want to pin.

3 Tap Pin To Start.

Tip

One quirk of Windows Phone: Games are the only apps that don't appear in the Apps list. You'll find them in the Games hub, under Collection, instead.

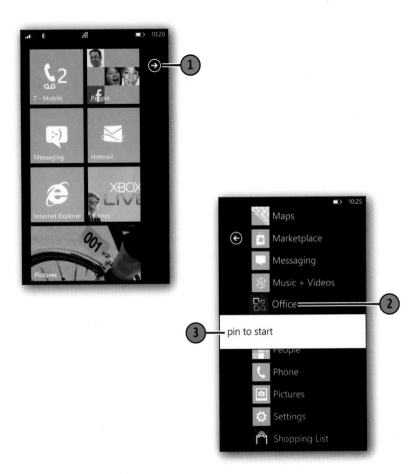

Changing Themes and Wallpaper

Windows Phone 7 provides lots of fun ways to make your phone reflect your unique personality or mood. One is by changing the phone theme. A theme is a combination of background shades and accent colors. Windows Phone comes with two backgrounds—light and dark—and 10 accent colors for things like tiles and text. Another way to add a personal touch is by customizing the lock screen wallpaper. You can use your own snapshot, or one of the artsy options that comes with Windows Phone.

Change the Theme

1. On the Start screen, flick left to the Apps list or tap the arrow.
2. Tap Settings.
3. Under System, tap Theme.
4. Do one of the following:
   - Tap Background to choose dark or light.
   - Tap Accent Color to choose a different color for tiles, links, and highlighted text.

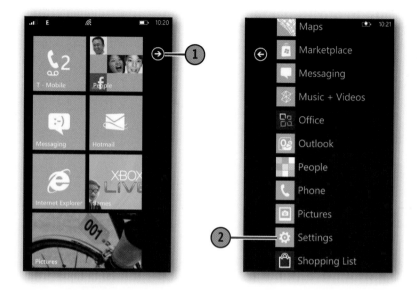

Change the Wallpaper

1. In Settings, under System, tap Lock & Wallpaper.

2. Tap Change Wallpaper.

3. Tap an album.

4. Tap a photo. If you choose one of your own, adjust the photo to your liking, and then tap Crop.

Picking Ringtones and Alerts

You won't find any rooster calls, honking car horns, or snippets of '80s hip-hop on your Windows Phone. Depending on your perspective, that could be a blessing or a serious bummer. What you will find are some of the most singular sounds of any smartphone. To create the phone's sonic palette, Microsoft designers drew inspiration from some pretty far-out sources, including—get ready— traditional Japanese pottery. There are 30 ringtones to choose from. You can also customize the alert sounds your phone makes when a new e-mail, voicemail, or text arrives.

Customize Ringtone and Alerts

1. On the Start screen, flick left to the Apps list or tap the arrow.

2. Tap Settings.

3. Under System, tap Ringtones & Sounds.

4. Tap Ringtone, or tap an alert.

5. To preview a ringtone or alert, tap the Play icon. To select one, tap it.

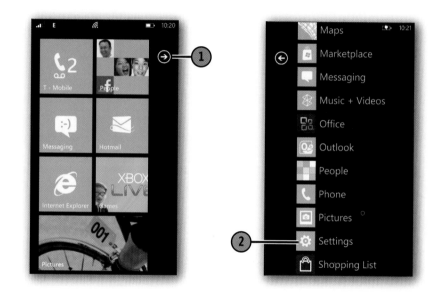

See Also

To learn how to give someone a recognizable ring, see "Adding a Picture or Ringtone to a Contact" on page 83. By assigning special ringtones, you don't even have to look at your phone to know who's calling.

Play

Tip

As of this writing, you can't create custom ringtones for your phone.

Tip

You can also choose whether you want your phone to play a sound for key presses, appointment reminders, and other notifications. Under Play A Sound For, select or clear the appropriate check box.

Silencing Your Phone

There's nothing like being on the receiving end of disapproving glares and not-so-subtle shushes when your phone sounds off in the wrong place—a meeting, a movie theater, the middle of a wedding. If you don't want to find yourself becoming "that guy" (or girl), but you still want to know about an incoming call, you have a couple of options.

Adjust the Volume

1. Press the Volume button on your phone to make it louder or softer. If you turn the volume down to 0, your phone goes into vibrate mode.

2. Or tap Ring to turn off the ringer and turn on vibrate mode. (If you've turned off vibrate mode in Settings, tapping Ring turns on silent mode instead.)

Change Ringer Settings

1 On the Start screen, flick left to the Apps list, and then tap Settings.

2 Under System, tap Ringtones & Sounds.

3 Do any of the following:

- Under Ringer, tap the slider to turn it off and stop your phone from making any sounds.

- Under Vibrate, tap the slider to make your phone silently notify you when a call or message arrives.

Tip

You can turn the ringer and vibrate mode on and off independently so that your phone can ring and vibrate, only ring, only vibrate, or play totally dead.

Importing Contacts from a SIM Card

A SIM card is the thumbnail-sized memory card found inside cell phones sold by AT&T, T-Mobile, and other carriers with GSM-based cellular networks. Along with basic information like your phone number, a SIM can store the names, addresses, and numbers of up to a couple hundred contacts. If you're swapping an old SIM into your new Windows Phone, you'll probably also want to import any address book info stored on the card. Luckily, it's easy to do.

Import Contacts

1. On the Start screen, flick left to the Apps list, and then tap Settings.

2. Flick to Applications, and then tap People.

3. Tap Import SIM Contacts.

Tip

The first time you visit the People hub, Windows Phone asks if you want to import contacts from your SIM card.

Caution

If you don't see the Import SIM Contacts option, it means you don't have any contacts to import or your Windows Phone doesn't have a SIM card inserted.

Locking Your Phone

The lock screen in Windows Phone is mostly designed to prevent you from accidentally brushing the touch-sensitive screen and dialing someone's number. But you can make it live up to its name by turning on the password-protection feature. Then you'll have to enter a four-digit code (of your choosing) to use the phone. That said, there are still some key things you can do when the phone is locked: answer a call, dial 911, or snap a quick photo, for example. The lock screen appears automatically if you haven't touched the phone for a short period. You can adjust how long.

Turn on Password Protection

1. On the Start screen, flick left to the Apps list, and then tap Settings.

2. Under System, tap Lock & Wallpaper.

3. Under Password, tap the slider to turn on password protection. If it's already on, you'll see a Change Password option. Tap it to enter a new secret code.

4. Do one of the following:

   - If this is your first time setting up a password, enter your new password in the New Password field, and then reenter it under Confirm Password.

   - If you're changing a password, enter the current password in the Current Password field and then enter the new four-digit code under New Password.

5. Tap Done.

Change Lock Screen Settings

① In Lock & Wallpaper settings, under Screen Time-Out, tap the menu and then choose a value between 30 seconds and 5 minutes.

② Press the Back or Start button to exit.

See Also

To learn how to personalize the photo that shows up on the lock screen, see "Changing Themes and Wallpaper" on page 26.

Tip

To make an emergency call when the phone is locked, just tap Emergency Call on the keypad and dial 9-1-1.

Tip

It's also possible to dial a number by voice when the phone is locked. Tap Settings > Speech, and then tap Use Speech When The Phone Is Locked. To learn more about what speech recognition can do, see "Talking to Your Phone" on page 54.

Finding a Lost Phone

Lots of people misplace their phone every year. Whether it's just under a couch cushion or you've left it behind at a store or restaurant, you can use a free online service to help get it back. Find My Phone, available online on Microsoft's Windows Live web portal, can ring your phone and show it on a map. If you think it's been stolen, you can also lock and erase the phone via the Web. Before you can use this service, you need to create a Windows Live ID on your phone or register an existing one.

Find, Lock, or Erase a Lost Phone

1. On your PC, go to windowsphone.live.com and sign in with the Windows Live ID you registered on the phone.

2. Click Find My Phone.

(continued on next page)

Find, Lock, or Erase a Lost Phone *(continued)*

3 Do one of the following:

- Click Map It to show your phone's approximate location on a map.

- Click Ring It to make your phone ring, even if the ringer is turned off or it's set to vibrate.

- Click Lock It to lock your phone. You can also post a message on the screen with your contact info.

- Click Erase It if you're convinced that you'll never get the phone back and want to make sure nobody can see what's on it or make unauthorized calls.

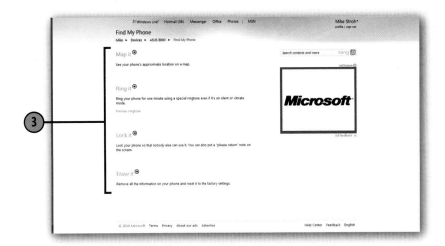

Updating Your Phone Software

Some smartphones receive their software updates over the airwaves. Windows Phone is designed to receive its software updates via the companion Zune software on your PC. You'll see a notification on your phone when an update is available. Just plug your phone into your PC, and Zune will do the rest.

Download an Update

1. Connect your phone to your PC via the USB cable, and then open the Zune software. (If this is the first time you are connecting your phone to your PC, you are prompted to install the software.)

2. In the Zune software, click Settings.

3. Click Phone.

4. Click Phone Update.

5. When the update is finished, click OK.

Tip ✓

Zune PC software isn't just for updates. See Section 16, "Synching with Your PC," starting on page 239, to learn more about how to use the Zune software to transfer pictures, music, and more to your phone.

Tip ✓

Although you use your PC to install updates, your phone can also let you know when they're available. Tap Settings > Phone Update to see or modify your notification settings.

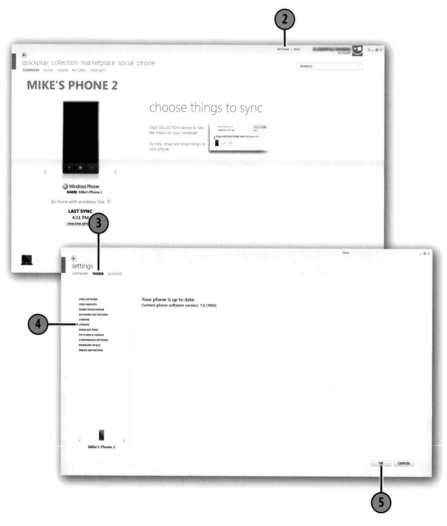

Turning On Airplane Mode

If you fly, then by now you've undoubtedly memorized the pre-takeoff spiel about turning off your cell phone and other electronic devices. The airplane mode setting in Windows Phone makes it easy to comply. When airplane mode is on, your handset's cellular, Wi-Fi, and Bluetooth radios are shut off, so they no longer emit any wireless signals.

Turn Airplane Mode On or Off

1. On the Start screen, flick left to the Apps list, and then tap Settings.

2. Under System, tap Airplane Mode.

3. Tap the Airplane Mode toggle to switch it on or off.

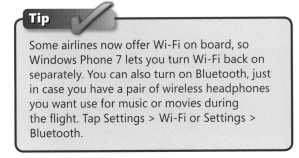

Tip

Some airlines now offer Wi-Fi on board, so Windows Phone 7 lets you turn Wi-Fi back on separately. You can also turn on Bluetooth, just in case you have a pair of wireless headphones you want use for music or movies during the flight. Tap Settings > Wi-Fi or Settings > Bluetooth.

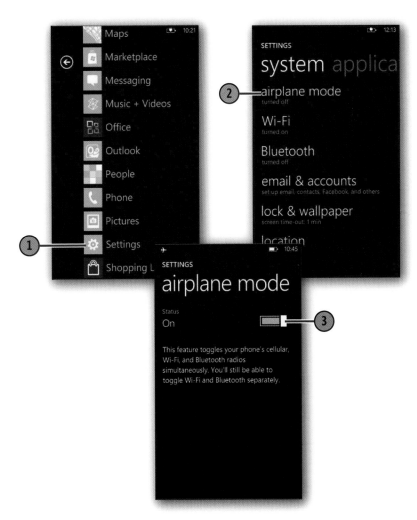

Connecting a Bluetooth Headset

Bluetooth is a wireless technology that lets you talk hands-free in your car—or look a little crazy in the supermarket. Bluetooth headsets typically have a range of roughly 30 feet, so you can stick your Windows Phone in a coat pocket, purse, or glove compartment and still make and take calls. The process of connecting a Bluetooth device is called *pairing*. Because using a Bluetooth device is a battery drain, your phone's Bluetooth radio is turned off by default. You know it's on when you see the little Bluetooth symbol in the status bar.

Add a Bluetooth Device

1 On the Start screen, flick left to the Apps list, and then tap Settings.

2 Under System, tap Bluetooth.

3 Tap the slider to turn on Bluetooth and search for nearby compatible devices.

4 When you spot your device in the list, tap it. Your device is paired automatically. Occasionally, you might have to enter a pairing code. If you don't know what to enter, check the device instructions.

5 Tap the device name again to disconnect the device.

Tip

You can delete a device from the list by pressing and holding your finger on its name and then tapping Delete.

Typing and Using Speech

Reviewers all pretty much agree on one thing: Windows Phone 7 has one of the best on-screen keyboards of any smartphone. And that's good news, because typing is one of the most basic and important tasks you do on your phone.

The keyboard, which appears any time you tap a text box, is tricked out with many ingenious, timesaving features. It can automatically add punctuation marks and capitalize words. It also has a beefy built-in dictionary for correcting typos and predicting what you're trying to type, which can save you taps. (Many of the time savers in this section apply even if your phone comes with a physical keyboard.) Microsoft engineers really paid attention to the small details. Some smartphone keyboards clickety-clack like a typewriter. Windows Phone makes no fewer than eight subtle typing sounds to fight monotony. (You can always turn the sound off.) In early 2011 Microsoft says it also plans to add copy and paste capability to the phone.

But the keyboard isn't your only input option. In this section, you'll also learn about the speech-recognition feature, one of the phone's hidden gems. Speech is a hands-free alternative to the keyboard and touch-screen for bread-and-butter tasks like making calls, opening apps, and searching the Web.

Exploring the On-Screen Keyboard

Don't be deceived by the flat, low-fidelity look of the on-screen keyboard. A lot of smarts lurk beneath its surface. The keyboard is laid out in a traditional QWERTY arrangement, with four rows of keys, and works whether you hold the phone vertically or horizontally (portrait or landscape views). The keys are slightly bigger in landscape view, and some people find typing easier that way. Experiment to see what works best for you.

As you'll quickly discover, the virtual keyboard is something of a chameleon: Depending on the app and what you're doing, its lineup of keys changes to make typing easier. This is most apparent in the bottom row. When you're typing an e-mail, for example, you'll see comma and happy face keys. But tap the To line, and now you see an @ key and a .com key instead, since those are more useful for entering recipient addresses.

Numbers and Symbols

There's really not one keyboard but many. Tap the &123 key to see the phone's palette of numbers, punctuation marks, and symbols. Tap the ABCD key to return to letter land. Curious about that happy face key? That's your gateway to emoticon heaven. (The cool thing about the emoticon menu is that it's quite international—some of the emoticons are more common in Asian or European countries than in the U.S.) Both the symbol and emoticon keyboards feature a More key that shows you yet another keyboard full of options.

Hidden Menus

But wait, as they say, there's more! Some keys conceal hidden popup menus, which you can see by pressing and holding a key for a moment. This is where Microsoft engineers stashed accents and other diacritical marks, like the Spanish ñ. Here you'll also find fractions, mathematical notations, and money signs. Granted, not everything is the stuff of everyday texting.

But when you need to note the temperature in degrees or communicate what something costs in euros, it's comforting to know you can.

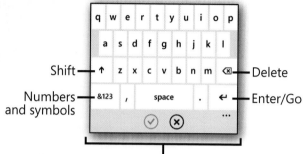

The on-screen keyboard in Windows Phone 7 is several keyboards in one

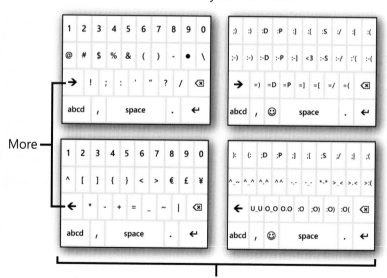

The More key toggles between keyboards with more options for symbols and emoticons

Finally, I want to draw your attention to a pair of hidden menus that can really save you time. Press and hold the period key to see a selection of other popular punctuation marks—the ones you see depend on the app or text box you're typing in. The .com key, meanwhile, also has common endings for Internet addresses, which saves you four whole taps.

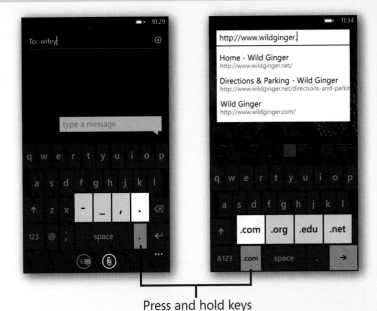

Press and hold keys to see more options

Press and hold this key	To type this
A	ä á â à å æ
C	ç ©
E	ë é ê è
I	ï í î ì
M	µ
N	ñ
o	ö ó ô ò œ ø
s	ß §
u	ü ú û ù
y	ÿ ý
1	½ ⅓ ¼
2	⅔ ²
3	¾ ³
0	°
.com	.org, .net , .edu
.	Varies
'	` "
"	« » " "
?	¿
-	_ ~ ¬ ·
)	] } >

Press and hold this key	To type this
(	[{ <
%	‰
$	¢ £ € ¥ €
!	¡
^	√
<	≤
>	≥
+	±
=	≠
|	¦

Typing Basics

Typing on the Windows Phone 7 virtual keyboard is pretty straightforward. Still, the keyboard might not always behave like the one on your PC, so it doesn't hurt to go over some of the basics.

Type a Letter

 To enter a letter, just tap it.

 To enter an uppercase letter, tap the Shift key. To turn on Caps Lock, press and hold Shift or double-tap it. Tap it again to turn Caps Lock off.

> **Tip**
>
> In some cases the keyboard knows enough to automatically capitalize a word—at the start of a new sentence, for example.

> **Tip**
>
> If you don't want to hear the keyboard's tapping sound, tap Settings > Ringtones & Sounds, and then clear the Key Press sound effect option.

Type a Number or Symbol

1. Tap the &123 key.

2. Find the number or symbol you want to type, and then tap it.

3. If you don't see the character you're looking for, tap the More key for additional options.

4. Tap the ABCD key to switch back to the alphabet.

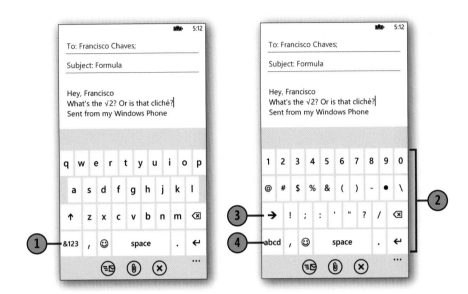

Editing Text

Two of the basic editing tools on the phone are the cursor and the Delete key. Delete has several gears—the longer you press it, the more it erases. The cursor—or *caret* as it's sometimes called—is useful for making surgical edits and cuts to something you've typed.

Place the Cursor

1 In the text box, tap and hold your finger until the editing cursor appears, drag it to the spot where you want to start editing text, and then lift your finger.

Delete Characters and Words

1 To delete something you've typed, use the Delete key in one of the following ways:

- Tap it once to erase a single character.

- Press and hold the key to erase multiple characters. If you hold the key long enough, it starts to delete entire words.

- Tap a word to highlight it, and then tap Delete.

Tip

Here's another trick for placing the cursor that's handy for longer words. Tap the word once to highlight it, and then tap it again to place the cursor. Depending on where you tap the word, the cursor shows up at the beginning or end of it.

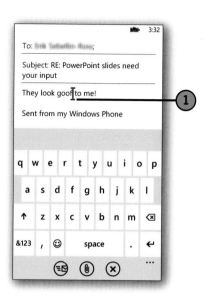

Working with the Suggestion Bar

As you type, Windows Phone 7 diligently cross-checks what you're typing against its dictionary and offers real-time suggestions and corrections. Suggestions can help you type more words in less time. If you misspell a word, the suggestion bar can also fix it for you automatically.

Use the Suggestion Bar

1 Start typing your message.

2 As you type, you'll see words fill the suggestion bar. Do any of the following:

- If you see the word you're trying to type, tap it. Flick the bar to see more suggestions.

- If the word in the suggestion bar appears in bold, tap Space to have Windows Phone automatically replace the word you just typed.

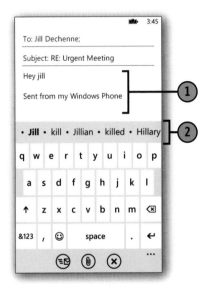

Fixing Mistakes

Windows Phone 7 can catch and fix a surprising number of common typos. For example, it automatically capitalizes the pronoun *I* and adds an apostrophe to contractions like *can't* or *won't*. The more you take advantage of these tricks, the faster you'll type. When Windows Phone doesn't recognize a word, it flags the suspicious entry with a squiggly red underline (only in e-mail and Word Mobile, however). You can always fix a goof manually, too.

Fix a Typo

 Tap the word you want to correct.

② If you see the word you want to replace it with, tap it. Flick left on the suggestion bar to see more replacement options.

Tip

Here's a big time saver: Tap Space twice at the end of any sentence. The phone not only adds a period but also automatically capitalizes the next word.

Tip

If you don't want Windows Phone to automatically suggest words, you can turn off suggestions by tapping Settings > Keyboard and clearing Suggest Text And Highlight Misspelled Words.

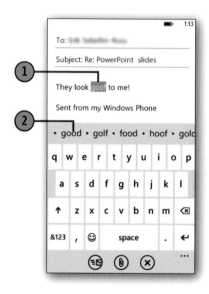

Customizing the Dictionary

The dictionary that comes with Windows Phone 7 is surprisingly comprehensive. (Case in point: Finding a word it didn't know for the screenshot you see below took a lot longer than I expected!) It even includes common first names, places, and abbreviations. Still, you'll undoubtedly stump it from time to time, especially with specialized vocabulary and slang. But the phone's designers thought of that, and they made it easy to add words to the dictionary and expand its vocabulary.

Add a Custom Word

1 Tap the word you want to add to the custom dictionary.

2 In the suggestion bar, tap the plus sign (+) to add the word you typed to the dictionary.

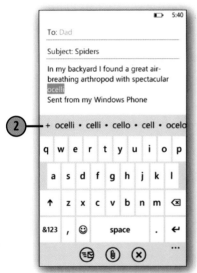

See Also

To learn how to erase all the custom entries from your phone's dictionary, see "Changing Keyboard Settings" on page 52.

Tip

Here's another sign of the intelligence in Windows Phone: When you add a word to the dictionary, it shows up prominently on the suggestion bar only if you use it frequently. If you don't use it much, it starts to fade in the rankings.

Changing Keyboard Settings

The things I find handy about the on-screen keyboard you may find annoying. No matter. Windows Phone lets you turn on or off many of the autocorrection features. You can also erase any words you've added to the dictionary.

Change Settings

1. On the Start screen, flick left to the Apps list.
2. Tap Settings.
3. Under System, tap Keyboard.
4. Do one of the following:
   - Select or clear any of the check boxes for settings you want to change.
   - To clear your suggestion list, flick down and tap Reset Text Suggestions.

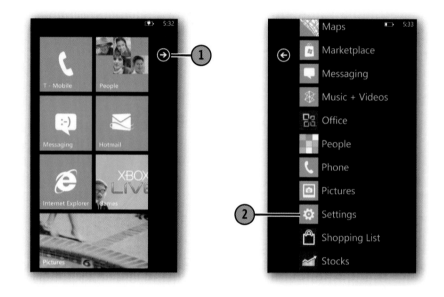

Talking to Your Phone

The touch-sensitive screen might be the primary way you interact with your phone and order it to do things. But it's not the only way. Windows Phone also comes with a nifty speech-recognition feature that lets you tell your phone what to do. Speech, as the feature is known, isn't well advertised—it's hidden behind the Start button. But it can come in handy when your hands are full or you can't afford to look down at the screen for long periods (like when you're driving). The speech feature also works with Bluetooth headsets.

To do this	Say this
Dial a contact	"Call <contact name>" or "Call <contact name> <phone type>" (for example, "Call Dad mobile")
Dial a number	"Call <phone number>" or "Dial <phone number>"
Search the Web	"Find <search term>" or "Search for <search term>"
Open an application	"Open <app>" or "Start <app>" (works for Maps, Music + Videos, and others)

Tip

You can use speech recognition even when your phone is locked. Tap Settings > Speech, and then check Use Speech When The Phone Is Locked.

Use Speech

(1) Press and hold the Start button on your phone.

(2) When the Speech window appears, give your phone a command to dial a contact or number, open an app, or search the Web. (You have to tap Speak the first time you use it.)

(3) When you finish talking, tap Go or pause silently for a moment.

Tip

You can also cancel the request by tapping anywhere outside the Speech dialog box.

Tip

If you're in a noisy place, it might help to tap Go when you're done giving a command to the phone.

5
Talking on the Phone

Here's a shocker: Some people still actually want to make plain old telephone calls on their smartphones. (Hey, anything's possible.) The good news is that there's a reason Microsoft called it Windows Phone: Because, in addition to its skills as a web browser, media player, and pee-wee Xbox, it's also great for making and taking calls.

At a glance, Windows Phone 7 tells you who's calling (complete with headshot, if you like), how many calls you've made or missed, and whether a voicemail awaits. You can juggle multiple callers and painlessly cobble together conference calls.

Although Microsoft has stated that it eventually hopes to partner with all major U.S. carriers, at launch Windows Phone 7 is available only on GSM networks used by carriers such as AT&T and T-Mobile. If Windows Phone someday becomes available on rival CDMA networks, used chiefly by Verizon and Sprint in the U.S., it's possible that some of the calling features described in this section might look or work a little bit differently. We'll just have to wait and see.

Dialing a Number

It doesn't get any more old-school than this. Imagine that someone's handed you a business card, or you've scribbled down a phone number that's on a for-sale sign. Now you want to dial it. As you'll discover, you can make a call in Windows Phone 7 in multiple ways—including by voice. But even on a cutting-edge smartphone, sometimes it still comes down to tapping out the digits one by one.

Dial Using the Keypad

1 On the Start screen, tap Phone.

2 Tap Keypad.

3 Tap the number you want to call.

4 If you make a mistake, tap Delete to erase the digit.

5 After you enter the number, tap Call.

6 To hang up, tap End Call.

Tip

If you want to make an international call, press and hold 0 on the keypad until a + sign appears. Now you don't have to enter an international access code, just the country code, area code, and phone number.

See Also

To learn how to connect a hands-free device for making calls, see "Connecting a Bluetooth Headset" on page 40.

Tip

To add a number you've entered on the keypad to your contacts list, tap Save.

Tip

If you need to make an emergency call when your phone is locked, just tap Emergency Call on the lock screen keypad.

Calling Your Contacts

It's no accident that when you tap the Phone tile on the Start screen, you're taken directly to call history. Most of us talk to the same people again and again, so in Windows Phone, call history serves as a de facto favorites list; and it's often the easiest way to speed-dial friends and family. You can also dial someone from their contact card in the People hub.

Dial from Call History

① On the Start screen, tap Phone.

② In Call History, flick to the number or person you want to dial, and then tap Call.

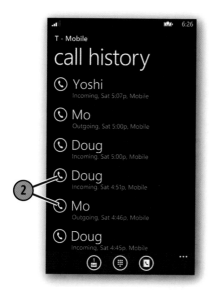

See Also

To learn how to turn off your cellular, GPS, Wi-Fi, and Bluetooth radios, see "Turning On Airplane Mode" on page 39. Airplane mode is useful when you're flying or to save battery power.

Tip ✓

Press the Search button to search call history for a caller or number.

Dial from a Contact Card

① On the Start screen, tap People.

② Flick through the contacts list, and tap the person you want to call.

③ Tap the phone number you want to dial.

See Also

To learn how to dial phone numbers or contacts by using the phone's built-in speech recognition feature, see "Dialing by Voice" on page 62.

Tip

If you have a lot of contacts, press the Search button on your phone while in the People hub to quickly find the person you want to call.

Dialing by Voice

Windows Phone 7 comes with a built-in voice recognition feature that lets you tell your phone (among other things) who you want to call. The feature works right out of the box without any special setup or training. Voice dialing makes it easy to dial either a number or a contact without looking down at your phone—handy when you can't afford to be distracted. Efficiency enthusiasts take note: Of all the different ways to call someone in Windows Phone, this method is the only one that requires but a single tap.

Dial By Voice

(1) Press and hold the Start button for a few moments to open Speech.

(2) Do any of the following:

- Say "Call" or "Dial" followed by the number.

- Say "Call" or "Dial" followed by the name of someone in your contacts list. If the person's listing has multiple numbers, you can add "Mobile" or "Home" to specify one. For example, "'Call Alan Brewer Work.'"

(3) Tap Go, or just stop talking for a few seconds.

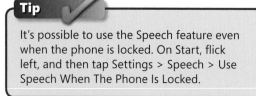

Tip

It's possible to use the Speech feature even when the phone is locked. On Start, flick left, and then tap Settings > Speech > Use Speech When The Phone Is Locked.

Answering Calls

When somebody calls, Windows Phone displays the number of the incoming call (provided it's not private). If the person or company is already on your contacts list, you might also see the caller's name and even their picture. Too busy to take the call? With a tap you can send it straight to voicemail.

Answer a Call

1 To pick up an incoming call, tap Answer. (If your phone is locked, you have to slide the lock screen out of the way first and then tap Answer.)

2 To send a caller directly to voicemail, tap Ignore.

3 When you finish talking, tap End Call.

See Also

To learn about adding a picture and unique ringtone for people in your contacts list so that you can quickly recognize them when they call, see "Adding a Picture or Ringtone to a Contact" on page 83. See "Silencing Your Phone" on page 30 to learn how to turn on vibrate mode so that your phone doesn't ring when somebody calls.

Juggling Calls

What happens if you're on a call and a new one comes in? You can ignore it and let voicemail pick up, or you can bounce between callers. Windows Phone can put one person on hold while you talk to the other. You can switch back and forth by tapping the top of the screen.

Switch to Another Call

1. If another call comes in while you're talking to someone, tap Answer. Windows Phone puts the first caller on hold and picks up the incoming call.

2. Or tap End Call+Answer to hang up on the first caller before answering the incoming call.

3. To switch between callers, tap the On Hold notification at the top of the screen.

Tip

Tap Ignore to send an incoming caller directly to voicemail.

Making Conference Calls

Windows Phone is also capable of the kind of advanced calling tricks once found only on fancy corporate office phones. Case in point: conference calling. While you probably won't have much occasion to use this feature outside work, it's still sometimes fun to get a bunch of old friends on the line for a virtual reunion. Windows Phone lets you add as many people to a call as your carrier allows.

Set Up a Conference Call

1. While on a call, tap the arrow, if necessary, to show in-call options.

2. Tap Add Call. Windows Phone puts the person or people you're talking to on hold and opens Call History.

3. In Call History, add another person to the call by doing one of the following:

   • Tap Call next to someone's name.

   • Tap Keypad, enter a number, and then tap Call.

   • Tap People, tap the person you want to call, and then tap a number to dial.

4. When the person answers, tap Merge Calls. To add more people, return to step 2.

5. To end a conference call, tap End Call. This ends the call for everyone.

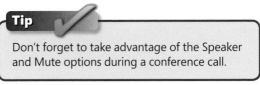

Tip

Don't forget to take advantage of the Speaker and Mute options during a conference call.

Speak Privately with Someone

(1) While on a conference call, tap the arrow, if necessary, to show in-call options.

(2) Tap Private.

(3) Tap the name or number of the person you want to speak with privately. Windows Phone puts everyone else on hold, so they can't hear your conversation.

(4) When you finish speaking privately, tap Merge Calls to resume the conference call.

(5) Or tap End Call to hang up on the person.

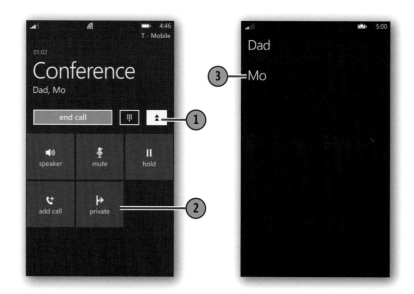

Tip

How many callers can you simultaneously have on a conference call? Theoretically, as many as you want. In practice, carriers often cap the number of people. Ask your carrier for more specifics.

Caution

Be sure to check the fine print on your service contract to see how your carrier charges for conference calls, so you don't inadvertently burn through your monthly minute allotment.

Using Speakerphone, Mute, or Hold

Windows Phone offers several convenient options while you're on a call. You can put a call on speakerphone when you've got your hands full—or when you want others in the room to join the call (perfect for a group rendition of "Happy Birthday," for example). Mute and hold, meanwhile, can provide a little temporary privacy.

Change In-Call Options

1. While on a call, tap the arrow icon to show the in-call options.

2. Tap Speaker to put someone on speakerphone. Tap it again to turn speakerphone off.

3. Tap Mute to turn off your microphone so that nobody else can hear you. (You're still able to hear what other callers say, however.)

4. Tap Hold to temporarily block both parties from hearing each other. Tap it again to stop holding.

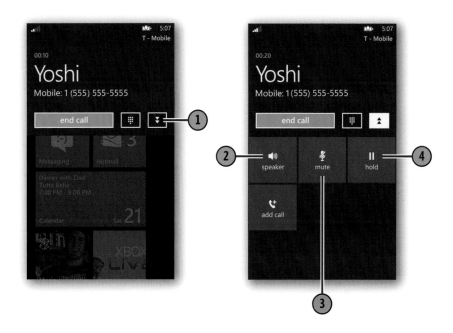

Managing Call History

Windows Phone records your last 300 calls, making it easy to track your incoming, outgoing, and missed phone traffic. It's also easy to clean up this list when it becomes too unwieldy.

Delete a Call

1. On the Start screen, tap Phone.
2. Press and hold the entry in call history you want to delete.
3. Tap Delete Item.

Delete All Calls

1. In Call History, tap More to open the menu.
2. Tap Delete All. In the confirmation dialog box, tap Delete.

Saving a Phone Number

If you receive a call from someone who's not in your contacts list, but should be, you can add the person's number directly from Call History. You can also do this when dialing a number.

Save a Number

(1) In Call History, tap the call entry you want to add to your contacts list.

(2) Tap Save.

(3) In Contacts, do either of the following:

- Tap New Contact to create a new contact card and add the number to it.

- Tap an existing contact to add the number to that person's card.

(4) When you finish adding the number, tap Done.

(5) Edit the contact card as needed.

(6) Tap Save.

Checking Voicemail

If someone leaves you a voicemail, you'll know because you'll see the little upside-down eyeglasses icon in the lower-left corner of the lock screen. The icon also appears on the Phone tile on Start. Setting up your voicemail box should be fairly straightforward. If you run into problems, consult your carrier's website or the information that comes with your phone.

Listen to Your Messages

1 On the Start screen, tap Phone.

2 Tap Voicemail.

3 Using the keypad, enter your password.

4 Follow the voice prompts to access any messages in your mailbox.

Tip

You can find the phone number for your voicemail box in Phone Settings. On Start, tap Settings > Applications > Phone.

Tip

You can also direct-dial your voicemail box by pressing and holding the 1 key on the keypad.

Forwarding Calls

You can set up your phone so that it automatically forwards calls you receive to another number. This can be handy if your battery is about to die and you want to send callers to a landline instead, or if you're going to be away without your phone.

Forward a Call

① On Start, flick left to the Apps list, and then tap Settings.

② Flick to Applications, and then tap Phone.

③ Tap Call Forwarding to turn it on.

④ Enter the number you want to forward your calls to.

⑤ Tap Save.

⑥ Press the Back or Start button to exit.

Changing Caller ID Settings

You might not want to show your phone number to every Tom, Dick, or Harry. Maybe just Tom and Harry. Windows Phone 7 gives you that option. When you hide your number from someone, all they see is "Private" when you call.

Hide Your Number

1. On Start, flick to the Apps list, and then tap Settings.

2. Flick to Applications, and then tap Phone.

3. Under Show My Caller ID To, tap one of the following:

   • Everyone

   • No One

   • My Contacts

4. Press the Back or Start button to exit.

6 Connecting with People

Contact lists are pretty standard stuff on cell phones today. But the People hub in Windows Phone 7 is something different altogether. Part address book, part social networking app, People makes it easy to keep track not only of contact details, but also posts on Facebook or Windows Live.

When you add an e-mail or a social network account to your phone, all your contacts or friends from those services are automatically added to People. These contact "cards" are tappable. For example, enter someone's cell phone number, and you can call or text them on that number just by touching it. Same goes for street and web addresses. Touch one, and up pops the Maps app or Internet Explorer.

Like all hubs in Windows Phone, People is divided into sections: an A-to-Z list of contacts, a "recent" list of people you've interacted with lately, and an area called What's New. If you spend a lot of time on social networks like Facebook, you'll probably feel right at home in What's New, which offers a real-time feed of all your friends' posts and pictures. Feel the urge to post your own comment? That's possible from What's New, too.

Adding a Contact

Adding people to your contacts list is pretty straightforward. In Windows Phone 7 parlance, you create a new contact "card" with a person's details. This card isn't a static rundown like the Rolodex of old. After you enter information, you can interact with it: Tap a phone number to call it, an address to map it, or a website to browse it. The People hub makes it easier to stay in touch.

Add a Contact

1 On the Start screen, tap People.

2 Flick to All, and then tap New.

3 Do any of the following:

- Tap Name to add your contact's name, company, or title.

- Tap Account to choose an account to associate the contact with.

- Tap Phone to add a work, home, or mobile number.

- Tap Email to add one or more e-mail addresses.

- Tap Other to add details, including a street or website address, a birthday, an anniversary, a spouse or child's name, or a note.

4 When you finish adding a detail, tap Done.

5 Continue adding contact information as needed. When you finish, tap Save.

6 Press the Back or Start button on your phone to exit.

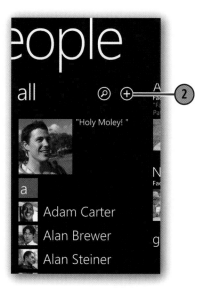

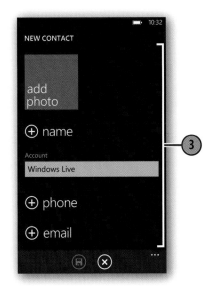

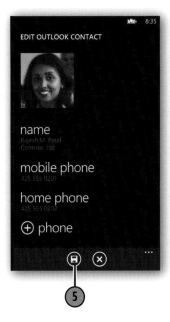

Tip

To call one of your contacts by voice, press and hold the Start button, and then say "Call" followed by the contact's name. If he or she has multiple numbers, you can add a clarifier like "Mobile" or "Home."

See Also

To learn how to add a headshot to a contact card or associate that person with a specific ringtone, see "Adding a Picture or Ringtone to a Contact" on page 83.

Finding a Contact

If you know a lot of people and they're all listed in your phone, flicking up and down your contacts list to find someone can grow tedious. But People offers two nifty tricks for giving your fingers a rest. You can jump to entries starting with a specific letter, and you can search for contacts by typing their name.

Use Quick Jump

(1) On the Start screen, tap People.

(2) Flick to all, and then tap any of the A-to-Z labels in the contacts list.

(3) Tap a letter to jump to that part of the alphabet.

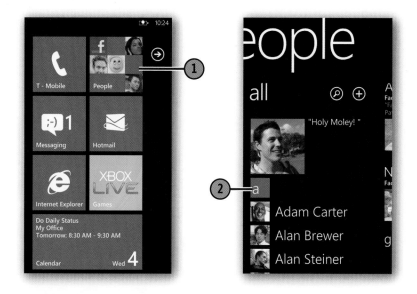

Use Search

① In the People hub, tap Search (or press the Search button on your phone).

② Tap the search box, and then start typing someone's name.

③ If you see a match, tap it.

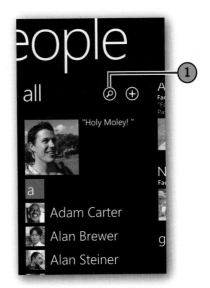

See Also

To change how names are listed or ordered in the People hub, see "Customizing Your Contacts List" on page 90.

Tip

If you set up a Microsoft Exchange (Outlook) account for your work e-mail, you can search your company address book by tapping the Search Outlook Directory option at the end of the results list.

Editing a Contact

If somebody in your contacts list changes jobs, moves to a new address, or adds a new cell phone number or e-mail address, you need to update his or her info on your phone. Here's how to do it.

Edit a Contact

① On the Start screen, tap People.

② Tap the name of the person whose details you want to edit.

③ Tap Edit.

④ If you are editing a linked contact, choose an account. Then do one of the following:

- To edit an existing field, tap it, enter the updated information, and then tap Done.

- To add a new field, tap the Add icon, enter the new information, and then tap Done.

⑤ When you finish, tap Save.

⑥ Press the Back or Start button on your phone to exit.

> **Tip** ✓
>
> You can't edit someone's Facebook information on your phone, but there's an easy workaround. Simply create a new contact card under a different account (say, Windows Live or Gmail), and link it to the person's Facebook profile.

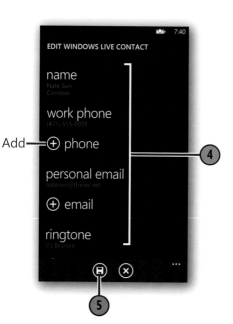

Add

Linking Contacts

Your coworker Joe is listed in your Outlook address book at work. He's also one of your Facebook friends. What happens if you add your Outlook and Facebook accounts to your phone? Two identical Joes in People? That would happen if Windows Phone didn't have a solution to the duplicate dilemma: linking.

When you link two or more contacts, you're declaring them to be the same person. Windows Phone consolidates the entries onto a single contact card. While linking contacts manually is easy enough, your phone is also designed to spot and link them automatically.

Link a Contact

① On the Start screen, tap People.

② Flick to All, and tap the contact you want to link.

③ Tap Link.

④ Do one of the following:

- If you see a match under Suggested Links, tap it.

- Otherwise, tap Choose A Contact, find the card you want to link, and then tap it.

⑤ Repeat the process to link another card, or press the Back or Start button to exit.

Tip

If you see a number in the Link icon, that tells you how many contact cards have been combined for this person.

Tip

What if someone has multiple profile pictures and names? You get to choose what details appear on the unified contact card for that person.

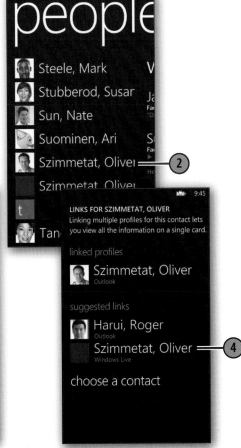

Unlink a Contact

1. In the People hub, tap the contact you want to unlink.

2. Tap Link.

3. Under Linked Profiles, tap the contact card you want to make separate.

4. Tap Unlink.

5. Press the Back or Start button to exit.

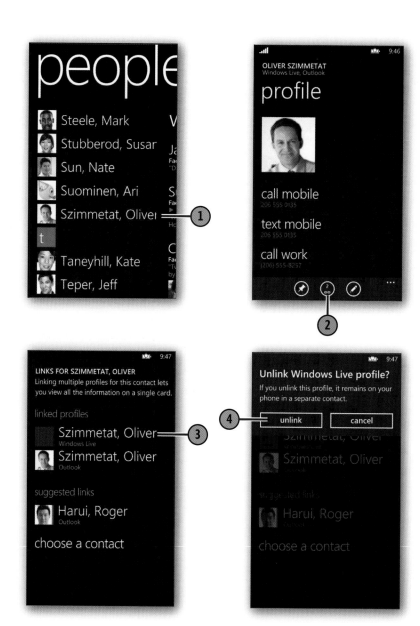

Deleting a Contact

When you delete a contact card, the information is removed from both your phone and the account the contact is associated with (except for Facebook contact cards, which can't be edited or deleted directly.) If the contact you're trying to delete has multiple linked cards, you have to specify which account profile to delete.

Delete a Contact

1. In the People hub, flick to All, and then tap the contact you want to delete.

2. Tap More.

3. Tap Delete. In the confirmation dialog box, tap Delete.

Tip

To delete a Facebook contact, you need to do it from your PC web browser.

See Also

To learn how to prevent all but your most important Facebook friends from showing up on your phone in People, see "Customizing Your Contacts List" on page 90.

Delete a Linked Contact

(1) In the People hub, flick to All, and then tap the contact you want to delete.

(2) Tap More.

(3) Tap Delete.

(4) Choose the account associated with the contact. When you see the confirmation dialog box, tap Delete.

See Also

To learn how to consolidate multiple contact cards for the same person through linking, see "Linking Contacts" on page 79.

Tip

You can also delete a contact by pressing and holding on the person's name in the People hub, then tapping Delete.

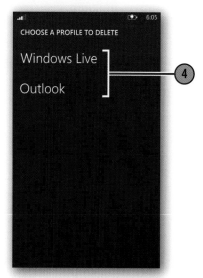

Adding a Picture or Ringtone to a Contact

Adding a picture to a contact card makes it easier (and more fun) to answer the phone. Windows Phone displays the picture whenever that person calls, so it's instantly clear who's on the line. Of course, if you assign a custom ringtone to a contact, you'll know who's calling before you even look at the phone.

Add a Picture

(1) On the Start screen, tap People.

(2) Flick to All, find and tap the contact you want to edit, and then tap Edit.

(3) Tap Add Photo, or if the person already has a photo, tap to change it.

(4) Do one of the following:

- In Pictures, find and tap the picture you want to use, adjust it if necessary, and then tap Crop.

- Tap Camera to take a picture of the person. If you like the result, tap Accept.

(5) Add other details to the card if you like, and then tap Save.

Tip

Sometimes adjusting a picture slightly can make for a better headshot. Drag the picture around with your finger to reposition it. Pinch or spread your fingers on the screen to zoom out or in.

Add a Ringtone

① In the People hub, find and tap the contact you want to update, and then tap Edit.

② Tap Ringtone.

③ To preview a ringtone, tap Play.

④ Flick up or down to see more options. When you find a ring you like, tap it.

⑤ Tap Save.

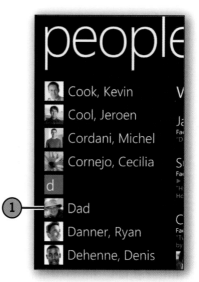

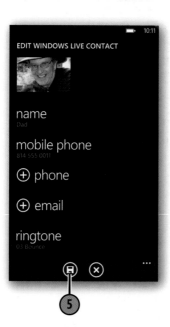

Pinning a Contact to Start

Any contact you connect with regularly is a good candidate for pinning to the Start screen. Pinning is the smartphone equivalent of speed dial: It lets you call or text that person with just two taps.

Pin a Contact

(1) On the Start screen, tap People.

(2) Flick to All, find the person you want to pin, and tap their name.

(3) Tap Pin.

Tip

You can also pin a contact to Start by pressing and holding the person's name in the People hub, then tapping Pin To Start.

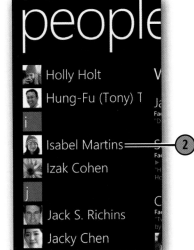

Posting to Facebook or Windows Live

If you're a fan of social networks like Face-book or Windows Live, you'll appreciate how easy it is on Windows Phone to keep up with your friends' posts and status updates or respond to them. Once you add an account, you'll see all your friends' posts in the What's New area of People.

Read or Comment On a Post

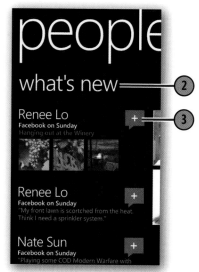

(1) On the Start screen, tap People.

(2) Flick to What's New.

(3) If you see a post you want to comment on, tap Comments.

(4) Tap the text balloon, and start typing your comment.

(5) When you finish, tap Post.

Tip

Tap Like to let someone know you liked what he or she had to say. If you change your mind later, tap Unlike.

Tip

The number inside the Comments balloon tells you how many people have left comments on that post.

See All Posts from a Contact

1 In the People hub, find the name of the contact whose posts you want to read, and then tap it.

2 Flick to What's New.

3 Flick up or down to scan the posts, or tap Comments to add a remark to one.

Tip

If you want to be sure you're seeing the latest posts, press and hold an empty spot on the screen, and then tap Refresh on the menu.

Tip

If you want to remove Facebook information from your phone, tap Settings > Email & Accounts. Tap and hold the Facebook account, and then tap Delete.

See Also

To learn how to post your photos to social networking services, see "Saving Pictures to the Web" on page 192. See "Setting Up Facebook" on page 20 to learn how to set up a Facebook account. You can have only one Facebook account on your phone at a time.

Working with the Me Card

The Me card in Windows Phone 7 shows all of your recent status updates, as well as messages and pictures posted to Windows Live or your Facebook Wall. The Me card is handy if you forget what you said or want to see if somebody responded to you with a comment. The Me card also makes it easy to change your profile picture or status across multiple networks simultaneously.

Update Your Status

1. On the Start screen, tap Me.

2. Tap the status area to the right of your profile picture.

3. Tap the text box, and type a message.

4. Select the social network you want to update by tapping a check box.

5. Tap Post.

Tip

To see the most current postings in Me, tap and hold the screen, and then tap Refresh.

Update Your Profile Picture

① On the Start screen, tap Me.

② Tap your current profile picture.

③ Do one of the following:

- In Pictures, browse to the picture you want to use, adjust if necessary, and then tap Crop.

- Tap Camera to take a picture of yourself, and then tap Accept.

④ Select the social networks you want to update by tapping a check box.

⑤ Tap Post.

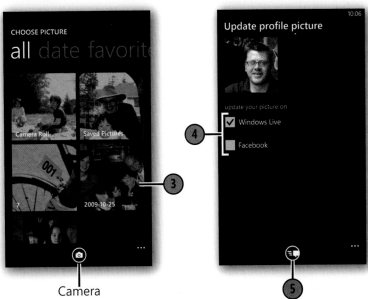

Camera

Customizing Your Contacts List

In Windows Phone 7, you have some control over how your contacts list looks. For example, you can change how you sort or display names. You can also filter out all but your most important Facebook friends by electing to show only people who already have a contact card on your phone.

Hide Facebook Friends

1 On the Start screen, flick to the Apps list, and then tap Settings.

2 Flick to Applications, and then tap People.

3 Under Include Facebook Friends As Contacts, tap Only Add Facebook Info To Existing Contacts.

4 Press the Back or Start button on your phone to exit.

Caution

This option affects only the contacts list. It doesn't affect the posts shown in What's New. Also, when you search People, you might see Facebook friends who are hidden.

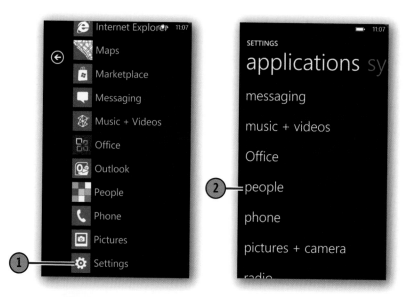

Change Sorting Style

(1) In Settings, flick to Applications, and then tap People.

(2) Do one of the following:

- Under Sort List By, choose whether you want the list sorted by a person's first or last name.

- Under Display Names By, specify how you want your contacts to be listed.

(3) Press the Back or Start button on your phone to exit.

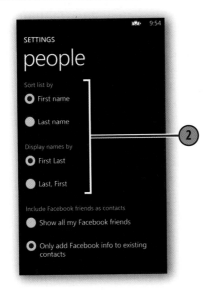

7 Reading and Sending E-Mail

Even in the age of Facebook and Twitter, e-mail remains vital for staying in touch and getting work done. In fact, these days it's not uncommon for people to own not just one address, but a whole slew of them—one for work, maybe a throwaway account for blog posts and Craigslist, and a private one for family mail.

If that sounds familiar, you'll be happy to know that Windows Phone 7 makes setting up and juggling multiple inboxes easy. The phone supports popular web-based service like Yahoo Mail, Google Gmail, and Windows Live Hotmail. It's also work friendly. If your company uses Microsoft Exchange Server to dish out e-mail—and many companies do—you can read and respond to mail and meeting invitations on your phone. You can also set up multiple Exchange accounts.

The Mail app in Windows Phone 7 is actually a mobile version of Microsoft Outlook, and it has many of the conveniences you're used to on the desktop. It can handle attachments and HTML mail. You can move or delete multiple messages, show only unread or flagged mail, or pinpoint specific ones with the Search button. E-mail is also made for multitouch: if you find yourself squinting, just use your fingers to zoom in or out.

Reading Mail

When new mail lands in your inbox, you'll know it. On the Start screen tile for your e-mail account, you'll see the number of unread messages you have. Windows Phone can also play a little ditty to announce each arrival (or not). Your inbox is easy to skim. Windows Phone displays the sender, subject line, and first sentence of each message. Unread mails are displayed in bold so you don't miss them.

Open a Message

① On the Start screen, tap an e-mail account.

② Tap the message you want to read.

③ Tap an arrow to see the next or previous message.

④ When you finish, press the Back button on your phone to return to your mailbox.

Tip

Windows Phone tries to make useful information in a message tappable. Try tapping a phone number to call it, a street address to map it, or a web address to see it in Internet Explorer.

Tip

Having trouble reading a mail? Spread your fingers on the screen to zoom in; pinch them together to zoom out. Scroll around by dragging your fingertip across the screen. This is especially handy for HTML mail.

Tip

If you want to make an e-mail message appear as though you never opened it, tap More > Mark Unread.

Sorting and Searching Your Mail

The Mail app in Windows Phone 7 comes with powerful tools that make it easier to find and filter mail. For example, you can hide messages that aren't important or that you've already read. The Search button on your phone, meanwhile, can pinpoint specific e-mails—handy when your inbox is brimming over.

Sort Your Messages

1 On the Start screen, tap an e-mail account.

2 Flick left or right, or tap a heading such as All, Unread, Flagged, or Urgent to show only those messages.

Search for a Message

1 In Mail, press the Search button on your phone.

2 Tap the search box, and then type the words you want to find.

Tip

Windows Phone searches the From and Subject fields, as well as the first 256 characters of the message body. As of this writing, Windows Phone is not capable of searching the entire body of a message.

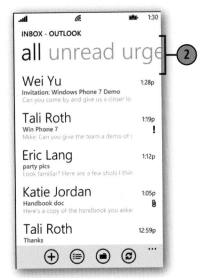
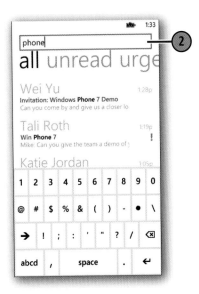

Checking for New Messages

By default, Windows Phone checks for new mail automatically. How often it checks depends on the account. The default for web accounts is every 30 minutes. Exchange accounts, on the other hand, are usually configured to deliver—or "push"—a message to your phone the instant someone sends it. But

there's a tradeoff to timeliness: The more frequently your phone checks for new messages, the more battery power it uses up. If you don't like the default automated schedule, you can easily change it—or manually sync your mail any time you like.

Check Manually

① On the Start screen, tap an e-mail account.

② Tap Sync to check for new messages.

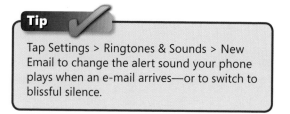

Tip

Tap Settings > Ringtones & Sounds > New Email to change the alert sound your phone plays when an e-mail arrives—or to switch to blissful silence.

Change Sync Settings

(1) On the Start screen, flick left to the Apps list or tap the arrow.

(2) Tap Settings.

(3) Tap Email & Accounts.

(4) Tap the account you want to change.

(5) Do any of the following:

- Tap Download New Content to change how often your phone checks for mail. You can download mail instantly as it arrives or as seldom as every hour. You can also turn off auto sync.

- Tap Download Email From to change how many days' worth of mail you download to your phone at once. The default is three days.

- Under Content To Sync, tap a check box to select or clear it.

(6) When you're finished, tap Done.

Responding to a Message

Most of the time, responding to an e-mail is fairly straightforward. Windows Phone gives you the same options you're probably accustomed to on your PC. If you set up an Exchange account on your phone for work, you can respond to meeting requests and invitations in addition to e-mail.

Reply or Forward a Message

1. On the Start screen, tap an e-mail account.

2. Tap the message you want to reply to.

3. Tap Respond.

4. Do one of the following:
   - Tap Reply to respond just to the sender.
   - If there are multiple recipients on the To line, tap Reply All to send your response to everyone.
   - Tap Forward to send the e-mail to someone else entirely.

5. Type your response.

6. Tap Send.

Respond to an Invitation

(1) On the Start screen, tap an e-mail account, and then tap the invitation or meeting request.

(2) Tap Respond.

(3) On the menu, tap a response: Accept, Tentative, or Decline.

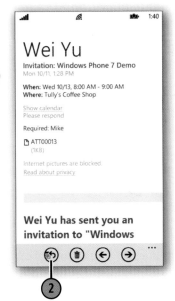

Composing a New Message

Reading e-mail is just half the equation. You'll also undoubtedly want to compose new mail on your phone. If you're using the on-screen keyboard to type your message, be sure to take advantage of all the tricks for typing faster found in Section 4, "Typing and Using Speech," starting on page 43.

Write an E-Mail

1. On the Start screen, tap the e-mail account you want to send from.

2. Tap New.

3. On the To line, do one of the following:

   • Type an e-mail address, and then tap Enter. Repeat as needed.

   • Type a contact's name.

   • Tap Add Contact to pick someone from your contacts list.

4. Fill in the Subject box, and type your message.

5. Tap More to see more message options:

   • Tap Show CC & BCC to send copies of the message to other people.

   • Tap Priority to let recipients know how important the message is: low, normal, or high.

6. When you finish, tap Send.

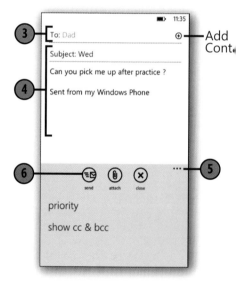

Tip

Cc stands for carbon copy. Bcc stands for blind carbon copy. Cc'ing somebody provides them a courtesy copy of your e-mail. Bcc'ing somebody hides that person's address from everyone on the To line—handy when you want to be discreet.

Tip

As you type in the To line, Windows Phone suggests matches from your contacts list. As soon as you see a match, tap it. If you accidentally enter the wrong person's name, just tap the name, and you'll see an option to remove it.

Saving a Draft Message

If you're busily tapping out a message to someone and suddenly need to map an address, you can save the message to your drafts folder and pick up where you left off later. That way you don't lose anything you've written.

Save a Draft

① In an open message, tap Close.

② Tap Save to preserve the message in your drafts folder.

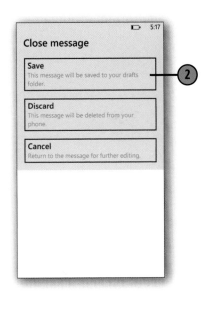

Tip

You also see these options if you press the Back button on your phone while you're composing a message. But you won't see them if you exit via Start.

Working with Attachments

A little paperclip icon lets you know that an e-mail has a file attached. You can open several types of files you receive in e-mail, including pictures, audio, videos, and documents. But—and this is an important caveat—you can send only two types of attachments from your phone: pictures and Microsoft Office documents. A file needs to be stored on your phone before you can attach it. So if you see a Facebook photo in the Pictures hub that you want to send to somebody, you need to save it to your phone first.

Attach a Picture

① On the Start screen, tap an e-mail account.

② Tap New.

③ Fill in the sender and subject information, and then write your message.

④ Tap Attach.

⑤ Do one of the following:

- Tap to open a folder, and then tap the picture you want to attach.

- Tap Camera to take a new picture. If you like the result, tap Accept to attach it.

⑥ Tap Send.

Tip

You can also send pictures from the Pictures hub by pressing and holding a picture, tapping Share, and then tapping the account you want to send your e-mail from.

See Also

To learn how to attach Office documents to messages, see "Sharing Documents via E-Mail" on page 225.

Camera

Open an Attachment

① In an e-mail with an attachment, tap the file name to download it.

② When the file has finished downloading, you'll see the icon change to indicate what type of attachment it is. Tap it to open.

See Also

To learn how to save a Facebook photo to your phone, see "Saving Pictures to Your Phone" on page 191.

Tip

To remove an attachment from an e-mail, tap Remove just below the attached file, and then tap Yes.

Managing Mail Folders

Most e-mail accounts have multiple folders. You probably have an inbox and an outbox and folders for drafts and junk mail. Maybe you even have a few custom folders. Sometimes mail folders need to be cleaned up and organized. Because Windows Phone lets you select multiple messages simultaneously, that's a fairly straightforward task.

Open a Folder

1. In Mail, tap Folders.

2. Tap the folder you want to open. If you don't see it, tap Show All Folders.

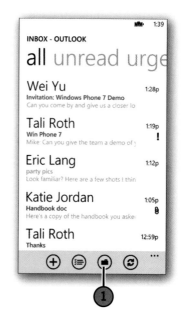

Moving and Deleting Messages

1 In Mail, tap Select.

2 Tap the check box to select the message you want to move or delete.

3 Do one of the following:

- Tap Move to move the selected mails, and then tap the folder where you want to move them.

- Tap Delete to delete the selected mails.

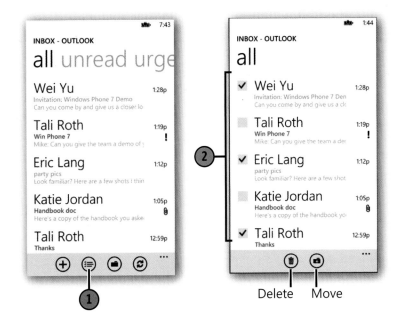

Delete   Move

Customizing Your E-Mail Signature

By default, your e-mails include the standard tagline "Sent from my Windows Phone." This e-mail signature, as it's known, is a good way to signal your Windows Phone pride. But it can also be useful. Recipients are less likely to expect an in-depth reply when they know you're replying on the fly from your phone. You can also add your own custom signature—or go signature free.

Edit Your Signature

1. On the Start screen, tap the e-mail account that you want to change.

2. Tap More.

3. Tap Settings.

4. Tap the check box to show or hide an e-mail signature.

5. Tap the signature text if you want to change it.

6. When you're finished, tap Done.

Deleting an Account

From time to time you might need to delete an account on your phone—if you change jobs or e-mail service providers, for example. Here's how to do it.

Delete an Account

(1) On the Start screen, flick left to the Apps list or tap the arrow.

(2) Tap Settings.

(3) Tap Email & Accounts.

(4) Press and hold the e-mail account that you want to delete.

(5) Tap Delete.

Caution

Windows Phone 7 requires you to have at least one Windows Live account on your phone. After you set one up, the only way to delete it is by resetting your phone to factory settings.

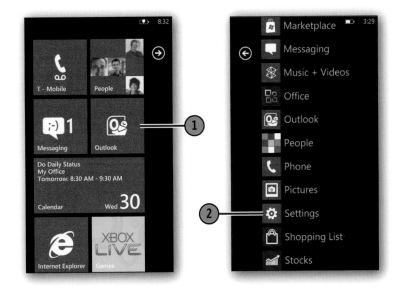

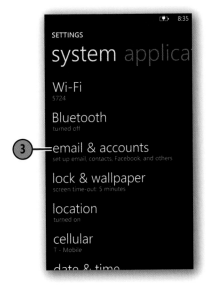

8 Sending Text Messages

Sending text messages—aka "texting"—was once a practice mostly associated with hard-charging business types and flirty teens. Some folks (guilty!) didn't understand what the big deal was. Flash forward to 2010: The tsunami of text and e-mail messages surging through U.S. cellular networks now surpasses voice calls. Texting has officially gone mainstream.

Text messages, it turns out, are pretty handy. Why? First, they're faster than e-mail. People might let an e-mail linger in their inbox for days, but they usually tap out a quick reply to a text. Texting is also less complicated than calling. Let's face it: Sometimes you don't feel like exchanging pleasantries just to find out who won the game. (The person you're calling might not either, frankly.) Texts offer an easy out. Finally, texts are silent. You can send or answer them in the middle of a movie or a meeting without disturbing the peace—provided you turn off new message alerts, that is.

In Windows Phone 7, text exchanges are fun and easy to follow: Your conversations play out comic-book style in dueling speech balloons, making it easy to pick up where you left off even days later. The phone also supports both traditional messages and messages with pictures or videos attached.

Opening a Message

Windows Phone 7 makes it easy to stay on top of incoming texts. The lock and Start screens show how many new messages you have waiting. The first few words of an incoming message also appear in the notification area at the top of your screen—which lets you see who's texting you and understand the gist of what they want. You'll also see one whimsical touch: The Messaging tile on Start changes expressions from a smile to a wink when a new message arrives.

Open a Message

1. On the Start screen, tap Messaging.

2. Tap the conversation you want to read. Conversations containing new messages are highlighted.

See Also

To learn how to change the jingle Windows Phone plays when a new text lands in your message box, see "Picking Ringtones and Alerts" on page 28.

Preview a Message

1. When a new message arrives, you see a snippet in the notification area at the top of the screen. You can tap it to go to Messaging and read the entire text. (Unless it appears on the lock screen, as shown here.)

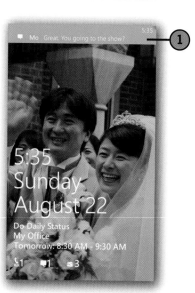

Sending a Message

Text messages are sometimes referred to as SMS messages, depending on who you're talking to and what part of the world you're in. SMS stands for Short Message Service, an allusion to the technology's nerdy early days and the fact that texts typically have a 160-character limit (about as long as this sentence). If you write a long message, Windows Phone automatically chops it up into multiple dispatches.

Create a New Message

1. On the Start screen, tap Messaging.

2. Tap New.

3. Tap the To box, and do any of the following:

   - Type a cell phone number or an e-mail address.

   - Start typing a contact's name. Windows Phone suggests matches. If you see one, tap it.

   - Tap Add to choose someone from your contacts list.

4. To add multiple recipients, tap Enter and repeat step 3. Otherwise, tap the message box and type your message.

5. When you're done, tap Send.

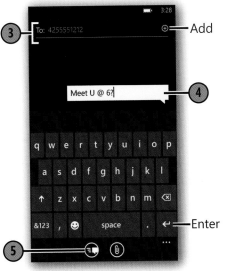

Add

Enter

Tip

If you add someone to the To line by mistake, tap his or her name and you'll see an option to remove it.

Tip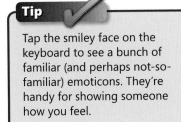

Tap the smiley face on the keyboard to see a bunch of familiar (and perhaps not-so-familiar) emoticons. They're handy for showing someone how you feel.

Reply to a Message

1 In Messaging, tap the conversation you want to respond to.

2 Tap the message box, and type your response.

3 When you're done, tap Send.

See Also

For tips on how to type faster and save time when texting, see Section 4, "Typing and Using Speech," starting on page 43.

Caution

Know your service contract. If you send a lot of texts and don't have unlimited sending privileges, charges can add up quickly.

Forwarding a Message

Once in a while, somebody sends you a text message that you just have to share. Maybe it's a side-splitting joke or a picture they snapped on their camera. Or maybe it's a message that contains an interesting web link or directions to the big party. In all these situations, the fastest way to let other people know about the text is to forward the message to them.

Forward a Message

① On the Start screen, tap Messaging.

② Tap the conversation that contains the message that you want to forward.

③ Press and hold the message you want to forward.

④ Tap Forward.

⑤ Tap the To box, and do one of the following:

• Type a cell phone number or an e-mail address.

• Start typing a contact's name. Windows Phone suggests matches. If you see one, tap it.

• Tap Add to choose someone from your contacts list.

⑥ If you want to add a message, tap the message box and type it.

⑦ Tap Send.

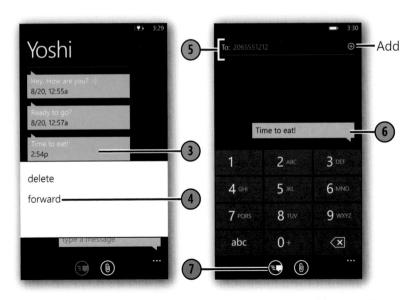

Adding Pictures to a Message

Newsflash: Texts aren't just limited to text. Windows Phone 7 also supports multimedia messages—a format known as MMS (Multimedia Messaging Service). For now, Windows Phone only allows you to send pictures via text. But you can receive messages containing pictures and videos. MMS messages are a great way to get someone's opinion on that dress you're thinking about buying or to instantly share your child's first home-run with a grandparent who lives faraway.

Send a Picture

1 On the Start screen, tap Messaging.

2 Tap New.

3 Tap the To box, and do one of the following:

- Type a cell phone number or an e-mail address.

- Start typing a contact's name. Windows Phone suggests matches. If you see one, tap it.

- Tap Add to choose someone from your contacts list.

4 Tap Attach.

5 Do one of the following:

- Find the picture you want to send, and then tap it.

- Tap Camera, take a picture, and then tap Accept.

6 Tap the message box and type a message if you want to include one.

7 Tap Send.

③ ———— To: Dad;   ⊕ ——— Add

CHOOSE PICTURE

date favorites

September 2009

March 2010

⑤

———— Camera

To: Dad;

I think you'll like this :-) ————— ⑥

⑦

④

Tip

Windows Phone 7 can handle most common picture file types, including JPEG, BMP, and PNG files.

Caution

The recipient must also have a phone that supports MMS messages.

Deleting Messages

If you let too many unread text messages pile up, the smiley face on the Messaging tile changes to a look of shock and dismay (really!). But it's easy to delete individual messages—or entire threaded conversations—with just a couple of taps.

Delete a Conversation

1. In Messaging, press and hold the conversation you want to erase.

2. Tap Delete on the menu. When you're asked for confirmation, tap Delete again.

Delete a Message

1. In Messaging, tap a conversation.

2. Press and hold the message you want delete.

3. Tap Delete on the menu. When you're asked for confirmation, tap Delete again.

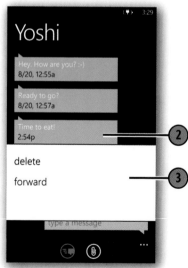

Adding a Sender to Your Contacts

If someone you just met sends you a text, you can add their information to your contacts list with a few taps. Then you'll see the person's name instead of just their phone number alongside incoming messages.

Add a Contact

(1) In Messaging, tap a conversation.

(2) Tap the phone number at the top of the thread.

(3) Tap Save.

(4) Do either of the following:

- To create a new contact card, tap New Contact.

- To add the number to an existing contact card, tap the name of the person.

(5) Make any changes to the phone number or number type.

(6) Tap Done.

(7) Fill out the other fields in the contact card as needed, and then tap Save.

9

Working with the Calendar

Most smartphones today come with some sort of calendar. But the one in Windows Phone 7 separates itself from the pack in a couple of important ways. First, it supports multiple calendars and shows all your goings-on in a single view—pretty nice if you have an active work and personal life. To make entries easier to tell apart, they're color-coded by calendar. Finally, both the lock screen and Start screen show details of your next appointment, so you'll always know where you're supposed to be.

Windows Phone 7 works with any calendar that supports Microsoft's Exchange ActiveSync technology, and most of the popular online ones, such as Windows Live and Google, do. Exchange ActiveSync is also common in the workplace. If you use Microsoft Outlook at the office, for example, you can manage your appointments and meeting invitations with just a few taps. Any changes you make on your phone are automatically synched to your online or desktop Outlook calendars and vice versa.

Working with the Calendar

The Calendar app has three views: Day, Agenda, and Month. The Calendar is "sticky," so whatever view you used last is the one you'll see the next time you open the app.

- **Day view**   This view provides a precise accounting of your day by dividing it into hour-long chunks. It's the easiest way to see how busy—or free—you'll be that day.

Tap or flick to switch views

Calendars are color-coded

Flick up or down to see a different day

Tap to see more details or edit

Appointment status bar

Tap for more menu items

Show today

Add a new appointment

Show the current month

- **Agenda view**   Shows your day as an appointment list. Agenda view hides days and time slots that don't have anything scheduled, making it ideal for quickly browsing your upcoming appointments.

- **Month view**   Shows the calendar month. You can't make out any daily details in this view, but you'll know which days you have plans.

Tap to pick a different month or year

Agenda view

Flick your finger up or down to see the previous or next month

Tap a specific date to see it in Day or Agenda view

See Also

To learn how to set up your calendar accounts on your phone, see "Setting Up E-Mail and Your Calendar" on page 18.

Adding Appointments

Once you set up a calendar account on your phone, entering a new appointment is fairly painless. Most of the boxes in the new appointment form are self-explanatory. Whatever changes you make on your phone show up on your web-based or Outlook work calendar and vice versa.

Create an Event

① On the Start screen, tap Calendar.

② Tap New.

(continued on next page)

When you see this	It means
▨	You haven't accepted the meeting request or have only tentatively accepted.
▮	You've agreed to attend this meeting, and the time is marked as busy on your calendar.

When you see this	It means
▯	A time slot is free.
⤧	In Agenda view, identifies a meeting conflict, or two appointments scheduled at the same time.

Create an Event *(continued)*

3 Tap a box to fill in any of the following:

- Tap Subject to enter the purpose of the event or meeting.

- Tap Location to indicate where it takes place.

- Tap Account to choose which calendar to add the event to.

- Tap When to specify the date and time.

- Tap How Long to specify the time span or to make the entry an all-day or multiday event.

4 Tap More Details for other options, and then do the following:

- Tap Status to show a time on your calendar as free, tentative, busy, or out of office.

- Tap Reminder to have Windows Phone alert you of a pending appointment.

- Tap Occurs to create a recurring event or appointment.

- Tap Private to make the appointment details visible only to you (handy for surprise parties or stealth job interviews).

5 When you finish, tap Save.

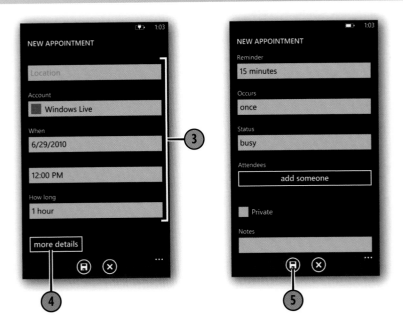

Tip

You can also create a new appointment by tapping an empty time slot in Day view.

Tip

If you're going on vacation, tap Custom under How Long to block off your calendar between specific dates. All-day appointments show up at the top of the calendar.

Editing Appointments

Picnics get postponed, and meetings change rooms to accommodate a larger crowd. In other words, your day is always a work in progress. If you ever need to update an invitation or correct the details of an event listed on your calendar, you can do it with a few taps.

Edit an Appointment

① On the Start screen, tap Calendar.

② Tap the appointment you want to change.

③ Tap Edit.

④ Update any of the appointment details by tapping the appropriate box and entering the new information.

⑤ When you finish, tap Save.

Tip

You can choose whether you want a sound to play for appointment reminders. To turn this option on or off, tap Settings > Ringtones & Sounds, and then tap the Appointment Reminders check box.

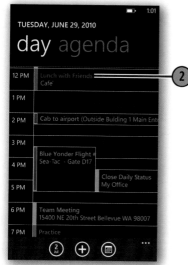

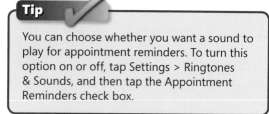

Deleting Appointments

Deleting appointments from your calendar is also pretty straightforward—just make sure that if you delete a recurring appointment, you don't accidentally remove all instances from your calendar (unless that's what you intended).

Delete an Appointment

1. In Calendar, tap and hold the appointment you want to delete.

2. On the menu, tap Delete. (When the confirmation message appears, tap Delete again.)

3. For a recurring appointment, tap One to delete only the current entry. Tap All to delete the entire series.

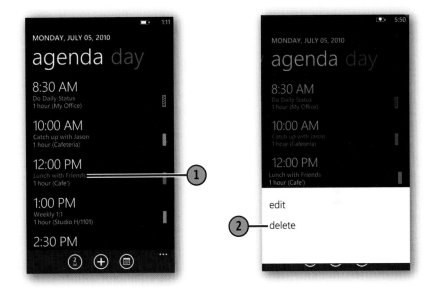

Changing Calendar Views

As I mentioned earlier, the Calendar has three main views: Day, Agenda, and Month. But there's also a Details view that shows you more specifics about an appointment. You can browse each view simply by flicking your finger on the screen. If you accidentally stray too far from the present day, the Calendar app can transport you back with a tap.

Show Day, Agenda, or Month

 In Calendar, you can see your upcoming appointments by doing one of the following:

- Tap Agenda to see your appointments as a list.

- Tap Day to see your appointments in a timetable.

② Tap Month to see the current calendar month.

③ If you've flicked too far forward or backward in time, tap Today to return to the present.

Tip

In Month view, tap the month name to call up a date picker that lets you quickly jump to a different month or year.

Tip

If you want to see your schedule on a day in the distant past or future, switch to Month view and then tap the date.

Show Details or Attendees

1 In Calendar, tap an appointment.

2 Do one of the following:

- Tap or flick to Details to see more information about an appointment or event.

- For meetings, tap or flick to Attendees to see who else is invited.

Sending an Invitation

It wouldn't be a meeting or party if you didn't send invitations. The Calendar app in Windows Phone makes it possible to send invitations straight from your phone. It's your choice whether to make someone you invite required or optional, depending on how indispensible they are.

Create an Invitation

1 In Calendar, tap New.

2 Fill in meeting details such as time, place, and subject, as needed.

3 Tap More Details.

4 Under Attendees, tap Add Someone.

5 Under Required or Optional, tap Add Someone.

6 Tap a contact. (If the person has more than one e-mail address, you have to choose which one to use.)

7 Add more required or optional attendees, as necessary. When you finish, tap Done.

8 Tap Save.

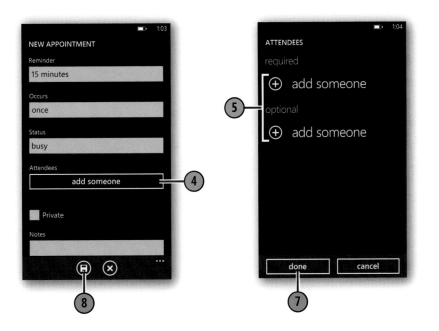

Tip ✓

If you set up a Microsoft Exchange account and want to add a coworker to an invitation who isn't in your contacts list, press the Search button, type the coworker's name, and then tap Search Outlook Directory to search your company directory.

Responding to an Invitation

If someone sends you an invitation to a meeting or party, you can quickly check your phone calendar and let the person know whether you can make it. You can even let people know when you're running a little late.

Accept or Decline an Invitation

1. On the Start screen, tap Calendar.

2. Tap the meeting invitation you want to respond to.

3. Do one of the following:

   - Tap Accept. (If it's a recurring appointment, then choose One or All.)

   - Tap Decline. (If it's a recurring appointment, then choose One or All.)

   - To tentatively accept, tap More, and then tap Tentative.

4. Add an optional comment with your response.

5. Tap Send. If you declined the invitation, it is removed from your calendar.

More

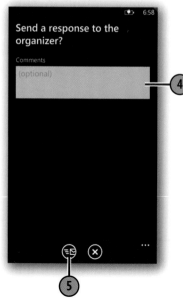

See Also

To learn how to accept or decline an invitation from your e-mail inbox, see "Respond to an Invitation" on page 99.

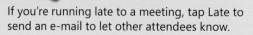
Tip

If you're running late to a meeting, tap Late to send an e-mail to let other attendees know.

Propose a New Time

(1) In Calendar, tap the meeting you want to reschedule.

(2) Tap Respond.

(3) Tap Propose New Time.

(4) Edit the appointment time, date, and other information as necessary, and then tap Done.

(5) Tap Send.

Juggling Multiple Calendars

If you set up multiple calendars on your phone, Windows Phone 7 shows each one in a different color so that it's easier to tell them apart at a glance. You can also customize the color or hide calendars. (You won't see these options if you have just one account set up.)

Change the Calendar Color

1. In Calendar, tap More.

2. Tap Calendars.

3. Under the calendar you want to change, tap the current color, and then tap a new color for that calendar.

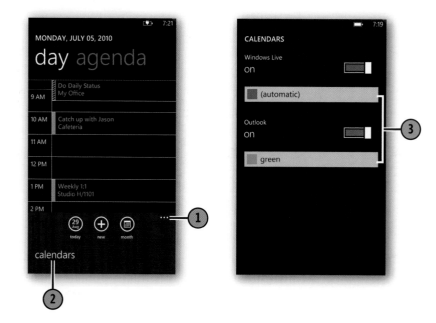

Hide a Calendar

① In Calendar, tap More.

② Tap Calendars.

③ Find the calendar you want to change, and then tap (toggle) the switch to turn it off. Tap it again to show the calendar.

10

Browsing the Web

If this is your first smartphone, it might come as a surprise just how easy it is to surf the Web on Windows Phone. The secret? Internet Explorer Mobile, a pocket-sized version of Microsoft's ubiquitous desktop web browser that's been tailored for touchscreen phones. The mobile version of Internet Explorer includes many of the conveniences found on its desktop cousin—such as the ability to open multiple browsing windows, bookmark your favorite websites, and save your browsing history so you can retrace your steps to a web page.

It also features buttery-smooth scrolling and zooming, so you shouldn't have a problem breezing through favorite newspapers, magazines, and blogs, even on the phone's smaller screen. (Case in point: I typically read the entire *New York Times* on the bus each morning on my phone.) While Internet Explorer Mobile doesn't carry over every bell and whistle from the desktop version—it doesn't support popular web technologies like Flash and Silverlight, for instance—you probably won't miss them much. For the most part, what you see on your phone is still the Internet you know and love.

Browsing Basics

Once you learn a few tricks, you'll find that surfing on Windows Phone is as easy as doing it on your desktop. How Internet Explorer Mobile responds to finger gestures is similar to what you find elsewhere on the phone.

Navigating Around the Page

- **Flick**   Flick your finger across the screen in any direction to scroll the web page. The faster you flick, the faster the page scrolls.

- **Pinch and spread**   Spread your thumb and forefinger apart to zoom in on a web page. Pinch your fingers together to zoom out. These are the key moves you need for reading on your phone.

- **Double-tap**   Double-tap your finger on a page to automatically center and zoom in on that part of the page. Double-tap again to zoom out.

- **Rotate**   Turn your phone 90 degrees to change to landscape view, which can make some web pages easier to read. It can also make the on-screen keyboard easier to type on because the keys are slightly bigger.

Pinch to zoom out and make text smaller

Stretch your fingers to zoom in

Navigating from Site to Site

On Windows Phone, your finger is the mouse. When you run across an underlined or highlighted link on a web page, just tap it. The site it points to will open in your browser. (And that's not all. If you run across a phone number or street address on a site, you can also often tap those to dial or map them.)

You'll also quickly notice that there aren't any arrow icons for whisking you to the next or previous page, like there are on your desktop browser. So how do you do it? Press the Back button on your phone to return to the site you last viewed. There's also a Forward option hidden behind the menu at the bottom of the browser.

Portrait view

Landscape view

Turning your phone sideways makes some sites easier to read

Opening a Web Page

There are two ways to open a web page on your phone: tap a link or type the web address, also known as the URL. As you start typing, Internet Explorer starts guessing which site you're looking for, based on your saved favorites, browsing history, and sites other people are searching for—a big time saver!

Open a Web Page

1. On the Start screen, tap Internet Explorer.

2. Tap the address bar.

3. Start typing the web address. You can save time by leaving off the *http://www* part.

4. As you type, Internet Explorer suggests possible matches. If you see the site you're looking for, tap it.

5. Otherwise, finish typing, and then tap Go.

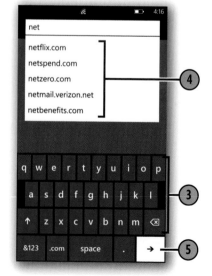

Tip

Turn your phone sideways so that the browser appears in landscape view. This view not only makes some sites easier to read; it also makes the on-screen keyboard slightly larger and easier to type on.

Tip

Press and hold the .com key on the keyboard to see other common web address suffixes, including .org, .net, and .edu.

Refresh a Web Page

① If you're browsing a web page that changes often, click Refresh in the address bar to update the information on the page. Refreshing a page can also help when the site doesn't load correctly.

Cancel a Web Page

① If a web page is taking too long to appear or you encounter some problem, tap Cancel in the address bar to stop the page from loading.

Caution

As of this writing, Internet Explorer Mobile doesn't support popular web technologies such as Flash. The upshot: Some web pages or videos might not look or work the way they do on your PC.

Browsing with Tabs

You probably already know how handy tabs are. Tabs let you keep multiple sites open at the same time so that you can bounce back and forth without the hassle of typing a web address. The good news is that Internet Explorer Mobile also offers tabs, and it lets you keep up to six sites open at once. Six is fewer than your PC browser allows, but it's plenty on a phone.

Open a New Tab

1. In Internet Explorer, tap Tabs.

2. Tap New to open a new browser window.

3. Tap the address bar, and start typing the web address. If you see the one you're looking for in the list, tap it.

4. Otherwise, when you finish typing, tap Go.

> **Caution**
>
> Smartphones are data gluttons. Be sure you're familiar with the terms of your service contract. Maybe you've heard tales of folks who mistakenly thought they had unlimited data plans—and wound up with a $10,000 phone bill? All true.

Switch Among Open Tabs

1. In Internet Explorer, tap Tabs.

2. Tap the tab you want to open.

3. To close a tab, tap the X icon.

Tip

If you see a number in the Tabs icon, it shows how many tabs you have open.

Searching the Web

Web searches are something most of us do, oh, only about a zillion times a day. Anticipating this need, engineers added a button to every Windows Phone that takes you straight to Bing, Microsoft's search engine. (Most of the time, that is. In certain apps the button is used to search for things on your phone, like contacts or e-mail.) What's great about having Bing on your smartphone is that it can take your location into account when providing search results. That means you can search both the Web and your immediate surroundings for, say, a place to eat or shop.

Search the Web

1. Press the Search button on your phone.

2. Tap the search box, and type the word or phrase you want to find.

3. As you type, Bing makes suggestions. If you see the search term you're looking for, tap it.

4. Otherwise, when you finish, tap Go.

5. Do any of the following:

   - Flick to Web to see the search results.

   - If you are searching for a local business, flick to Local to see any matches.

   - Flick to News to see news articles that include your search term.

Microphone

Tip

If you don't see local search results in Bing, you might need to turn on location services. Tap Settings, flick to Applications, and tap Search. Finally, tap Use My Location to turn on local search results.

Using Instant Answers

Bing also has a way-cool feature called Instant Answers that can provide you with answers to common questions you have when you're out and about, like what time is the next movie showing or when does the flight land?

Type "movies" to see what's playing near you

Type "weather" to check your local forecast

Enter a flight number to check the flight's status

If you want to find	Do this
Movies	Type **movies** to see everything playing in your area.
	Enter a theater's name to see what's playing there.
	Search for a specific movie to see starting times.
Weather	Type **weather**.
Stock quotes	Type a ticker symbol; **MSFT**, for example.
Flight status	Type a flight number; **UA102**, for example.

Understanding the Mobile Web

As you start to hop around to your favorite websites, you might notice that some look different on your phone from what you're used to seeing on your PC. Probably they look a lot simpler. In fact, some sites *are* different on a phone. Welcome to the Mobile Web.

Many popular news and shopping sites have mobile versions, including Amazon.com, MSN, and CNN. These stripped-down sites are primarily designed to make the Web easier to digest on slower cell connections and the primitive browsers found on basic cell phones. It's a great idea—and on an older phone it can mean the difference between having some Internet access or none at all.

But in recent years cell networks have gotten faster, and smartphones such as Windows Phone come with browsers that rival the ones found on desktop PCs. Some sites, however, can't distinguish between a smartphone equipped with a powerhouse browser (like the one you're using) and the primitive browsers on a basic cell phone. The result? Every phone gets served the stripped-down version of a site.

There are ways around this. If you look closely, you'll find that some mobile sites have a link to the desktop version. Windows Phone also provides a way to make your website preference known. In Settings, under Internet Explorer, you'll find a desktop or mobile option. Once you select this setting, most sites you visit will oblige.

Desktop version of Amazon.com

Mobile version of Amazon.com

See Also

To learn how to specify which kind of site you want to use, see "Setting Your Website Preference" on page 154.

Saving a Favorite Site

Some people think of them as bookmarks. Microsoft calls them favorites. No matter the term, marking the sites you routinely visit saves you a lot of time and tapping later. You don't have to retype the address; just look for it in your favorites list.

Add a Site to Favorites

① In Internet Explorer, open the website you want to save.

② Tap Add.

③ Internet Explorer automatically fills in the name and web address (URL) of the site. If you want to edit an entry, tap its text box.

④ Otherwise, tap OK.

Tip

If Internet Explorer fills in a name that's too long or generic, change it to something that's shorter or makes more sense to you.

Open a Saved Favorite

① In Internet Explorer, tap Favorites.

② Flick to the site you want to open, and then tap it.

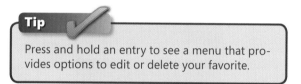
Tip

Press and hold an entry to see a menu that provides options to edit or delete your favorite.

Pinning a Website to Start

If there's a website that you visit often, consider adding a short-cut to it to your Start screen—or, in Windows Phone parlance, pinning it there. Once you've pinned a site, you just need to tap the shortcut tile to open the site in Internet Explorer.

Pin a Website to Start

① In Internet Explorer, open the website you want to pin, and then tap More.

② Tap Pin To Start.

③ Next time you want to visit the site, just tap the shortcut on the Start screen.

You can change how the tile for your shortcut looks by zooming in or out or by repositioning the web page before you pin it.

Sharing Links

Sometimes you run across a website that you just have to let someone know about. In Windows Phone, you can accomplish that goal with a few quick taps by sending someone a link via e-mail or a text message.

Share a Link

1. In Internet Explorer, open the website you want to share, and then tap More.

2. Tap Share Page.

3. Choose how to share the link. Tap Messaging to send it via text message. Otherwise, tap an e-mail account you've set up.

See Also

To learn how to send a text message, see "Sending a Message" on page 111. See "Composing a New Message" on page 100 to learn how to send an e-mail message from your phone.

Saving Pictures from the Web

If you find a great picture on the Web—maybe on a friend's photo-sharing site—you can save it to your phone. Once the picture is saved, you can use it as your lock screen wallpaper or send it to someone in an e-mail or a text message.

Save a Picture

1 In Internet Explorer, press and hold your finger on an image.

2 Tap Save Picture. The image is placed in your Saved Pictures folder in the Pictures hub.

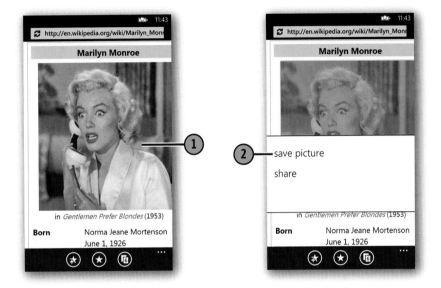

Tip

If you want to share a picture with someone via e-mail or text message, choose Share from the menu.

See Also

To learn how to change your lock screen wallpaper, see "Changing Themes and Wallpaper" on page 26.

Working with Browsing History

Internet Explorer keeps a list of every website you visit, which is handy if you ever want to revisit a site you've been to and can't remember its address. Deleting your browsing history is also easy if you're concerned about privacy or you just want to free up space on your phone.

Return to a Site

1. In Internet Explorer, tap Favorites.
2. Flick to History.
3. Flick through the list to the site you want to revisit, and then tap it.

Delete History

1. In Internet Explorer, tap Favorites.
2. To remove all the sites from your history, tap Delete. When the confirmation dialog box appears, tap Delete again.

Finding Text on a Web Page

It's often tricky to find a word on a website. This is doubly true when you're using a phone. But Internet Explorer Mobile can do the searching for you. Just type the word you want to find, and the browser will highlight any instances of it on a page.

Find Text

(1) In Internet Explorer, tap More

(2) Tap Find On Page.

(3) Type the word or phrase you want to find.

(4) Tap Return.

(5) Internet Explorer highlights any matches. Tap the Previous or Next arrow to see more matches on the page.

Changing Privacy Settings

Cookies are small files on your phone that websites use to remember things like your password or preferences, so you don't have to retype information each time you visit the site. If cookies make you uneasy, or you just want to clean house, you can remove them from your phone—or tell your phone not to save them in the future.

Delete Cookies and History

① On the Start screen, flick left to the Apps list, and then tap Settings.

② Flick to Applications, and then tap Internet Explorer.

③ Tap Delete History to erase browsing history, saved cookies and passwords, and temporary Internet files from your phone. When the confirmation dialog box appears, tap Yes.

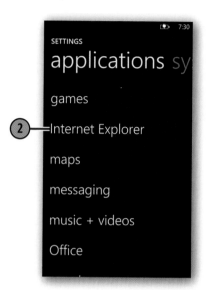

Turn Cookies On or Off

1 In Settings, flick to Applications, and then tap Internet Explorer.

2 Tap from to select or clear the check box.

Setting Your Website Preference

Many popular sites, like Amazon and CNN, offer slimmed-down versions of their sites designed specifically for phones. Some folks prefer these mobile sites, others don't. Internet Explorer lets you choose which type of site you want to see.

Set Your Site Preference

1. On the Start screen, flick left to the Apps list, and then tap Settings.

2. Flick to Applications, and then tap Internet Explorer.

3. Under Website Preference, tap Mobile Version or Desktop Version.

Caution

Websites don't always honor your request. You might still see the mobile version of a site even though you told Windows Phone otherwise. On the bright side, many mobile sites also have a link to the full version somewhere on the page.

Finding Places and Getting Directions

Every Windows Phone comes with a built-in GPS, so your phone should always know roughly where you are, even if you don't. The Maps app is a mobile version of Bing Maps, Microsoft's powerful online mapping and navigation service.

When you first open the Maps app, you don't see much. But don't be fooled by its Zen-like appearance. Maps is one of the handiest apps on your phone—one you'll come back to again and again. It can tell you where you are, find a place or an address, give you turn-by-turn directions, and show you how bad traffic is. Maps can even help you pick out a great place to shop or eat and show you what's on the surrounding blocks, so you can discover places you never knew existed.

Working with Maps

The map on your phone has multiple zoom levels. With a few moves of your fingers, you can change from a view that shows entire continents to one that lets you make out your neighbor's house and cars parked out front.

Moving Around the Map

Here's how to navigate the map:

- Flick your finger across the screen in any direction to move the map that way. The faster you flick, the faster the map scrolls.

- To zoom closer, spread your fingers apart on the map. To zoom out, pinch your fingers together.

- Double-tap the map to automatically center and zoom in on that spot. Double-tap again to get even closer.

How Does My Phone Find Me?

It's one of the almost-magical qualities of modern smartphones: their uncanny ability to locate you, just about any time or anywhere. To do this, Windows Phone 7 relies on three different techniques. The first and most accurate is GPS. By pinging the network of Earth-orbiting satellites that make up the Global Positioning System, the phone can narrow down your location to about 30 feet—or roughly the length of a school bus.

But a satellite fix can take time, and it isn't often possible when you're indoors. So Windows Phone tries to provide a quick guesstimate by using other means. One way is by sniffing around for a Wi-Fi signal. Every Wi-Fi access point has a unique network address. By comparing this address against a database of Wi-Fi access points, your phone can narrow down your location to about 325 feet.

Finally, there's the cell tower technique. By using the known locations of nearby cellular antennas, Windows Phone can pinpoint your whereabouts to within one-third of a mile, give or take. Outside big cities, cell towers can be spread farther apart. So, if you're in a rural area and Windows Phone can't get a satellite fix, it might be able to place you only within a mile or two of your actual location. But, hey, at least you'll know roughly which town you're in.

Aerial view

My location

Road view

Tap for more options

Get directions

Where am I?

Find address or place

Finding Yourself

No, I'm not trying to get new-agey on you. Knowing your precise whereabouts is obviously handy—and yet isn't it surprising how often we don't know? Your phone can help. Depending on what type of signal you have—GPS, Wi-Fi, or cellular—Windows Phone can typically narrow your location to at least

the nearest neighborhood (unless you're really in the middle of nowhere). Often you'll know to within a bus length or two. A circle on the map indicates the margin of error. Your actual location is somewhere inside the circle.

Show Your Location on a Map

1. On the Start screen, flick left to the Apps list or tap the arrow.

2. Tap Maps.

3. Tap Me.

 Tip

Is Windows Phone having trouble finding you? Don't worry, you're probably still somewhere on planet Earth. You've probably just temporarily lost your GPS or cellular signal.

Caution

The first time you open Maps, it asks you for permission to use your location information. Unless you're the paranoid type, there's nothing to fret about. Just tap OK.

Tip

If you use Maps frequently, you can save yourself time by pinning it to the Start screen. Press and hold the Maps tile, and then tap Pin To Start.

Finding Places and Things

This is the meat and potatoes of Maps: finding stuff. Of course, you can search for a specific address, but what you might not realize is that the Maps app can also handle a whole slew of other requests, including landmark and business names.

Find a Place

1. On the Start screen, flick left to the Apps list or tap the arrow.

2. Tap Maps.

3. Tap Search.

4. Tap the search box, and type any of the following:

   - An address (for example, One Microsoft Way, Redmond, WA)

   - A ZIP code (for example, 21230)

   - A city or town (for example, Erie, PA)

   - A business name or type (for example, McDonalds or sushi)

   - An intersection (for example, 42nd and Eliot)

   - A landmark (for example, the Golden Gate Bridge)

5. Tap Go.

6. Tap a black pushpin to learn more about a location or business.

See Also

To learn how to put a shortcut to a favorite address or location on the Start screen so its easier to map, see "Pinning a Favorite Place to Start" on page 168.

Combine search keywords to narrow your results. For example, type **pizza 98052** to see all the pizza places in the 98052 ZIP code.

Tip

If you're using your hands, you can search for an address or location by voice. Just tap the microphone icon in the search box.

Seeing What's Nearby

Tapping a black pushpin on the map calls up the About card for that location. Depending on the place, you might see a street address, phone number, web address, or business hours. In some cases Windows Phone also shows you customer reviews—handy if you're trying to decide where to shop or eat. Finally, the About card can show nearby shops and sights, a powerful time-saver if you're on vacation or in an unfamiliar part of town.

Get Place Details

(1) In Maps, search for a place or business, and then tap a black pushpin.

(2) Tap any of the highlighted details to, for example, get directions, dial a number, or open a website in Internet Explorer Mobile.

(3) Flick to Reviews to see what other people think about a place or location (if reviews are available).

(4) Flick to Nearby to see what else you'll find in that area.

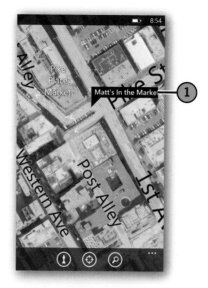

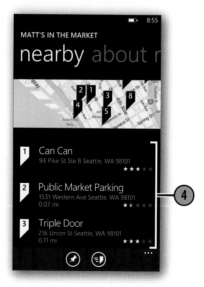

Finding Your Contacts

If you need to visit a friend's house or a business client, Maps can show you the address.

Find a Contact

① On the Start screen, tap People.

② Tap a contact.

③ Tap the address you want to map.

④ Tap the pushpin to get turn-by-turn directions from your location, if you need them.

Getting Directions

Getting from A to B (you've been to B, haven't you?) is a breeze. Windows Phone provides detailed, turn-by-turn directions to get you to your destination. It's important to note, however, that Windows Phone 7 only gives written directions. It doesn't bark orders at you the way some car navigation systems do. Still, it's pretty darn handy—and specific. It can tell you when something is "across from the 7-Eleven" and when you've gone too far.

Get Turn-by-Turn Directions

1. In Maps, tap Directions.

2. Tap the text box, and type one of the following:

   - An address

   - A business or landmark name

3. Tap Go.

4. Tap Walking or Driving to recalculate the route based on how you are traveling there.

5. Flick up or down the directions list, or tap a direction to see it on the map.

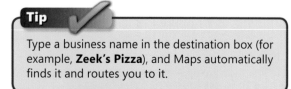

Tip Type a business name in the destination box (for example, **Zeek's Pizza**), and Maps automatically finds it and routes you to it.

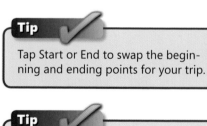

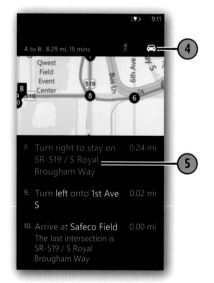

Tip Tap Start or End to swap the beginning and ending points for your trip.

Tip Maps assumes you want to start from your current location. To start from someplace else, tap My Location and enter another starting point.

Getting Real-Time Traffic Conditions

Windows Phone 7 can show you how clogged the roadways are, whether you need to tell someone you'll be running late, or maybe rethink your route home. Coverage is limited mostly to major roads, and the service isn't available in every city.

Show Traffic Conditions

① In Maps, tap More.

② Tap Show Traffic.

③ If Maps has traffic information for your city, it indicates traffic flow with four colors: green, yellow, red, and black.

When you see	It tells you traffic is moving at
Green	80 percent of typical speed or greater
Yellow	50–80 percent of typical speed
Red	25–50 percent of typical speed
Black	25 percent of typical speed or less

Caution

Traffic information isn't available everywhere. If you don't see anything when you turn on this feature, it's probably not available where you are.

Sharing an Address with Someone

Need to show someone where to meet you? Send the address directly to their phone or computer so that they can see it on a map or get directions. You can share an address via text message or e-mail.

Share an Address

① In Maps, tap the pushpin for the location you want to share.

② Tap Share.

③ Choose how you want to share the address:

- Pick Messaging to send it via text (SMS).

- Pick an e-mail account you've set up.

See Also

To learn how to send a text message to someone, see "Sending a Message" on page 111. For information about how to send an e-mail message to someone, see "Composing a New Message" on page 100.

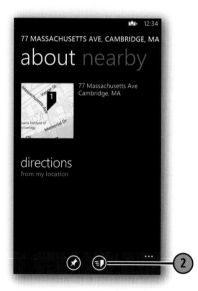

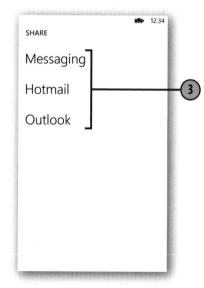

Changing Map Views

There's more than one way to look at a map in Windows Phone 7. You can see the map in traditional road view or from space by using aerial view. If you've just searched for a coffee shop or another popular business and have too many pushpins cluttering the screen, you can also switch to list view to make the map easier to read.

Show Aerial View

1. In Maps, tap More.

2. Tap Aerial View On. To return to road view, tap Aerial View Off.

3. Spread your fingers on the screen to zoom in closer. Pinch them together to zoom out.

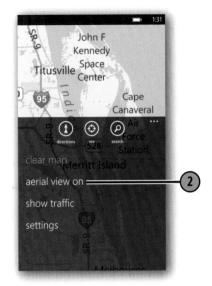

Show List View

1. In Maps, tap More.

2. Tap Results List.

3. Tap a listing to see more information about it.

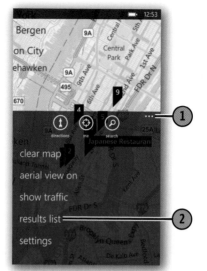

Adding a Pushpin

Windows Phone displays search results in Maps with pushpins But you can also stick your own pushpin on the map. Why do that? If you want to get directions to some place but don't know the exact address, find it on the map and then stick a pushpin there. Pushpins can also help you remember a place you want to visit or be used to share a meeting place with friends.

Drop a Pushpin

1. In Maps, flick to the spot where you want to add a pushpin. Press and hold your finger at the location until the pushpin appears.

2. Tap the pushpin to get directions to that location or to share it with someone.

Clear Pushpins

1. In Maps, tap More.

2. Tap Clear Map.

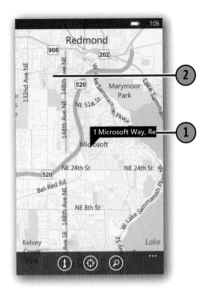

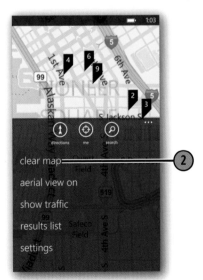

Pinning a Favorite Place to Start

You can pin places or businesses you love to your Start screen so that you can call or map them with a tap.

Pin a Place

1 In Maps, tap a pushpin on the map.

2 Tap Pin.

3 To see this location in the future, find its tile on the Start screen and tap it.

12 Playing Music and Video

The Music + Videos hub in Windows Phone 7 inherits much of its digital DNA from Zune, Microsoft's sleek line of portable media players. Never heard of Zune? Sadly, you're not alone. Zune is one of Microsoft's least-known consumer products—and is also considered one of its best by audiophiles, gadget connoisseurs, and fans of cool design. Go figure. The good news is that Microsoft engineers melded many of Zune's best features with Windows Phone 7, which means you get a twofer: a great phone and a first-class media player.

As with the rest of the phone, there's more to the Music + Videos hub than meets the eye. In this section I'll explore its secrets, showing you how to play music, TV shows, movies, and podcasts on your phone. You can play media either by copying it from your PC library or by buying it from Marketplace, Microsoft's virtual entertainment store. In fact, to get the most from the Music + Videos hub, I recommend reading this section alongside Section 14 (starting on page 201), which shows you how to shop on Marketplace, and Section 16 (starting on page 239), which explains how to copy media files to your phone from your computer.

What's Where in Music + Videos

When you first land in the Music + Videos hub, you'll see a main menu with five options: Music, Videos, Podcasts, Radio, and Marketplace. Flick horizontally across the hub, and you'll see two more areas: History and New. History shows you what you're playing now and what you've played lately. New reminds you of the music or videos you've synched to your phone or downloaded from Marketplace most recently.

Main menu

Tap items in History or New to play

Background in Music + Videos shows the artist you're playing

Play your entire music collection in random order

Shop for music to download, stream, or sample

What's playing now, including status and elapsed time; tap to switch to Now Playing view

Albums, videos, podcasts, or playlists that you've played most recently

New lists the most recent items you've added to your phone

Playing Music

It's easy to start playing music and to add more songs or albums to your song queue. You can even listen to music while you're doing other things on your phone—surfing the Web, checking mail, or looking for directions in the Maps app. If a call comes in while you're rocking out, Windows Phone automatically pauses whatever you're playing while you take it. Another sweet touch: The background in Music + Videos gets decorated with a picture of the artist you're playing.

Play Music

1. On the Start screen, tap Music + Videos.

2. Tap Music.

3. Flick left or right to browse the categories: Artists, Albums, Songs, Playlists, Genres. Flick up or down to browse within a category.

4. Tap the item you want to play.

5. Use the playback controls to play, pause, rewind, fast-forward, or change tracks.

See Also

To learn how to buy music, or stream and download it directly to your phone using a Zune Pass subscription, see "Shopping for Music" on page 210.

Tip

In a hurry? Tap the Play icon next to Music in the main menu to play everything in your collection in random order.

Add Tracks to the Now Playing Queue

① In the Music + Videos hub, tap Music, and then browse to the song, album, playlist, artist, or genre you want to add to your song queue.

② Press and hold the item.

③ Tap Add To Now Playing.

Tip ✓

To quickly find a song, an artist, or an album in your collection, tap one of the A–Z headers, and then tap a letter to jump to that section of your collection.

Caution !

If your phone is connected to your PC, you have to disconnect the USB cable before you can play or watch anything.

Controlling Music Playback

When you tap a song or an album, Windows Phone switches to the Now Playing view. You'll see playback controls and information such as the artist's name and picture, the album name, the song that's playing, and what's next in the playback queue. But there's also a lot you don't see, including hidden options to shuffle or loop the music, read an artist's bio and an album review, and search Marketplace for more music from the artist. If you navigate away from Music + Videos to, say, look something up on the Web, you can still use the mini-playback control to stop, start, and change tracks.

Control Playback

① In the Music + Videos hub, browse to the item you want to play, and then tap it.

② Do one the following:

- Tap Previous to return to the beginning of the track. Tap and hold to rewind it.

- Tap Pause to stop playing. Tap Play to resume.

- Tap Next to skip to the next track. Tap and hold to fast-forward.

③ Shows the current and next few songs in the Now Playing queue. Tap to see the complete list. (To hide the queue, wait a few seconds or press the Back button.)

④ Swipe left or right on the album cover to play the next or previous song in the Now Playing queue.

(continued on next page)

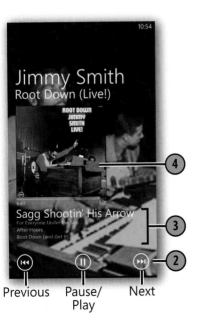

Previous   Pause/Play   Next

Control Playback *(continued)*

5 If you like, tap the album cover to see more playback options:

- Tap Repeat to play the songs in your song queue endlessly.

- Tap Shuffle to play the songs in your song queue in random order.

- Tap the heart icon to mark the song as one you like (filled heart) or don't like (broken heart).

6 Tap the artist's name to see more information, including a biography, a list of songs and albums by the artist on your phone, and what you'll find by the artist in Marketplace.

7 Press the Back or Start button to exit.

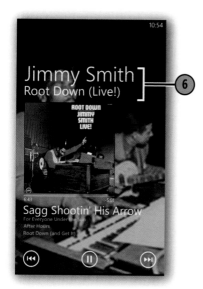

> **Tip** ✓
>
> If you want to let someone know about a great album in your collection, press and hold it and then tap Share to send someone an e-mail or a text message with your recommendation.

> **Tip** ✓
>
> You can see whether more music by the same artist is for sale in Marketplace. In the Now Playing view, press and hold the album cover, and then tap More In Marketplace.

> **Tip** ✓
>
> Why rate a song? One good reason is to have the Zune software sync only songs you like to your phone. In Zune, click Settings>Phone> Don't Sync Songs Rated (broken heart symbol).

Use the Mini-Playback Control

1 Press the Volume button on your phone to display the mini-playback control, which lets you pause, play, or change tracks when the phone is locked or when you're doing something else on the phone.

Tip

If you press the Search button within the Music + Videos hub, you'll search Marketplace, not the media collection on your phone. In Windows Phone 7, there's no direct way to search your media collection.

See Also

To learn how to copy music or videos in your PC multimedia library to your phone, see "Synching Media with Your Phone" on page 242.

Watching Videos

Every Windows Phone 7 comes with a high-resolution color screen that's perfect for catching up on missed episodes of your favorite TV shows, watching movies on a long flight, or replaying your favorite personal videos. Windows Phone is also capable of playing high-definition (HD) video, although the picture is scaled down to fit the screen. (So what you're watching isn't technically HD, but it should still look fantastic.)

Watch a Video

1. On the Start screen, tap Music + Videos.

2. Tap Videos.

3. Flick left or right to browse the categories: All, TV, Music, Movies, Personal. Flick up or down to browse items within a category.

4. Tap the video you want to watch. All videos on Windows Phone 7 play in landscape view.

5. To control playback, do one of the following:

   • Tap Previous to skip backward seven seconds. Press and hold Previous to rewind the video.

   • Tap Pause to temporarily stop playback. Tap Pause again to resume.

   • Tap Next to skip ahead 30 seconds. Press and hold Next to fast-forward the video.

6. Press the Back or Start button to exit.

Caution

If your phone is connected to your PC, you have to disconnect the USB cable before you can play or watch anything.

See Also

To learn how to record videos with your phone, see "Recording a Video" on page 190. See "Shopping for TV Shows and Movies" on page 206 to learn how to find TV shows and movies for your phone in Marketplace.

Tip

Double-tap the playback control overlay to see information about a TV show or movie.

Tip

When you are playing videos, tap the screen to make the playback controls reappear.

Playing Podcasts

Podcasts are audio or video programs that you can download to your PC and then play on your phone. The beauty of podcasts is that they can be created by just about anybody—and cover just about any subject under the sun. You'll find podcasts from major media outlets like NPR—and ones from undiscovered talents recording from their garage. Whatever your taste, you can find a great selection of podcasts to play on your phone in Zune Marketplace on your PC.

Play a Podcast

① On the Start screen, tap Music + Videos.

② Tap Podcasts.

③ Flick to choose an audio or a video podcast.

④ Tap the podcast title to choose an episode.

⑤ Tap the podcast image to start playing the most recent episode.

⑥ To control playback, do one of the following:

- Tap Previous to skip backward seven seconds. Press and hold Previous to rewind.

- Tap Pause to temporarily stop playback. Tap Pause again to resume.

- Tap Next to skip ahead 30 seconds. Press and hold Next to fast-forward.

See Also

To learn how to download podcasts from Marketplace to your PC and sync them to your phone, see "Subscribing to Podcasts" on page 212.

Listening to FM Radio

Did you know that your Windows Phone includes a built-in FM radio? That's right, you can tune in to your favorite station whenever the mood strikes you. Catch the news, listen to the game, or just get your groove on. To tune in your favorite stations more quickly, save them as presets. Or just pin a favorite station to the Start screen.

Tune In a Station

1. On the Start screen, tap Music + Videos.

2. In the Music + Videos hub, tap Radio.

3. Flick left or right to tune in a station.

4. Tap Presets to show your station presets.

5. To add the station as a preset, tap Add. To remove a station as a preset, tap Remove.

6. Tap Play to start listening. Tap Pause to stop listening.

Tip

You might see information on your phone about the station you're listening to, such as its genre and the name of the current song or program. Since it's up to the broadcaster to supply this information, you might not see it for every station.

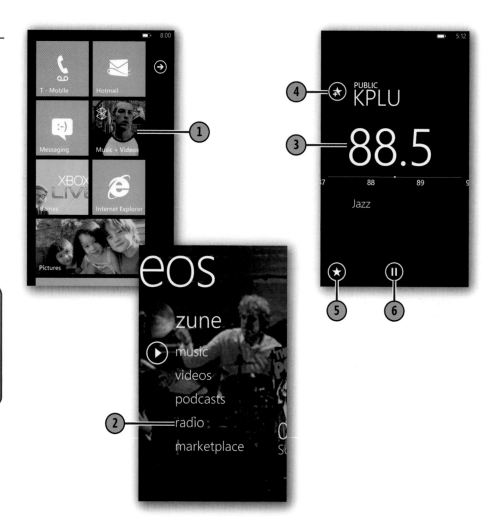

Choose an Audio Option

1 While playing a station, tap and hold the station number.

2 Tap Radio Mode: Headset or Radio Mode: Speaker to switch between the options.

Pinning Favorites to Start

If you really, really love a song and can't bear to have it out of your sight, here's a simple solution: Pin it to the Start screen. What can you pin? Just about anything in Music + Videos—even a radio station. Whenever you pin something, a tile for that item shows up on the Start screen.

Pin to Start

1. In the Music + Videos hub, browse to find the item you want to pin.

2. Press and hold the item until the menu appears.

3. Tap Pin To Start.

Deleting Music or Video

You can delete music, videos, or podcasts from your phone in two ways. You can do it on the phone itself, or you can do it on your PC. Remember that even if you delete something from your phone, you might still have a copy of it on your computer.

This can be a blessing if you accidentally get rid of something you actually wanted to keep. All you need to do is sync your phone with your computer.

Delete on the Phone

1 In the Music + Videos hub, browse to find the item you want to delete.

2 Press and hold the item until the menu appears.

3 Tap Delete.

See Also

To learn how to copy media files from your PC to your phone, see "Synching Media with Your Phone" on page 242.

Delete from the PC

① Connect your phone to your PC, open the Zune software, and then click Phone.

② Browse to the item you want to delete.

③ Right-click the item.

④ Click Delete From [*your phone name*].

Tip

To delete all synched music, videos, pictures, and podcasts from your phone at once, in the Zune software click Settings > Phone > Sync Options > Erase All Content.

13 Taking Pictures and Videos

Windows Phone 7 is a photo-lover's phone. From the start, one of Microsoft's goals was to make its new smartphone a credible alternative to your pocket point-and-shoot camera (because, really, who wants to carry both?). So all Windows Phones sport a minimum 5-megapixel camera. Microsoft engineers also wanted to avoid what they considered a weakness of other camera phones: they're too slow. On most phones, you have to tap open a camera app to take a picture, or waste precious seconds unlocking your phone. By then, you probably missed your photo op.

You'll miss fewer good shots with Windows Phone. Press and hold the Camera button for a few moments, and you go straight to shooting mode—even if the phone is locked or asleep. The camera includes other thoughtful innovations, like the ability to quickly review freshly taken photos and videos, so you know if one's a dud. Finally—and this is my favorite part—the phone features lots of creative and fun ways to showcase your shots. The lock screen and Pictures hub both let you decorate them with your photos. The Pictures hub can also pull in online photo albums from Facebook and Windows Live.

What's Where in the Pictures Hub

The Pictures hub is divided into three areas, which you browse by flicking left or right. First is a menu of options for displaying the pictures and videos on your phone. Tap All to see your collection organized by album. The Date option shows pictures and videos arranged by month. Favorites is where you'll find pics (sorry, no videos allowed) you previously earmarked as ones you like.

Flicking left past the menu takes you to the gallery, which displays a random selection of items from your collection. (The lineup, which changes every few visits, was designed for serendipitous pleasure, not practicality.) The last area in the Pictures hub *is* practical, however. What's New provides a handy photo feed from your Facebook and Windows Live accounts, if you have them.

Windows Phone 7 has two default albums: Camera Roll, where you'll find all the pictures or videos you take, and Saved Pictures, for photos you save to your phone. You can personalize the background image in the Pictures hub with one of your photos, which also shows up on the hub's Start screen tile.

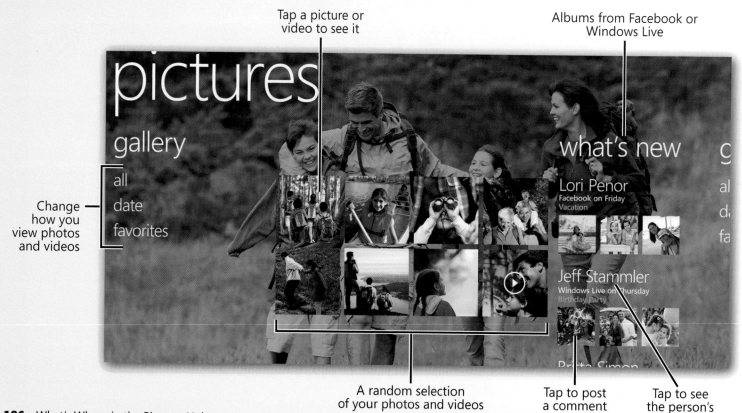

Tap a picture or video to see it

Albums from Facebook or Windows Live

Change how you view photos and videos

A random selection of your photos and videos

Tap to post a comment

Tap to see the person's contact card

Taking a Picture

Taking a picture is as simple as pressing the Camera button on the side of your phone (or wherever it's located on your model). As I mentioned, one of the things that really sets Windows Phone apart is how fast you can snap a photo. It doesn't matter if your phone is asleep or locked. Just press and hold the button for a few moments, and you're ready to shoot. Any pictures or videos you take on your phone are deposited into Camera Roll in the Pictures hub.

Take a Picture

1. Press the Camera button. (If your phone is asleep or locked, you have to press and hold the button.)

2. Tap to select camera mode.

3. If necessary, tap Settings to adjust the flash and other shooting options. (Options here vary by phone model.)

4. Tap the plus or minus sign to zoom in or out on your subject.

5. Press the Camera button halfway to focus the lens. Press it completely to take a picture.

6. After you take a picture, you can flick right to see how it turned out.

Tip

If pressing the Camera button doesn't wake up your phone, tap Settings > Pictures + Camera, and then make sure that Allow The Camera Button To Wake Up The Phone is turned on.

Tip

The first time you use the camera, Windows Phone asks permission to include location info with your photos. These so-called *geotags* can be handy, allowing you to see where a photo was taken on a map or sort your collection by place.

Tip

The first time you use the camera you're asked if you want to automatically share your pictures to Windows Live SkyDrive. See "Saving Pictures to the Web" on page 192 to learn more about this.

See Also

To learn how to add a headshot to a contact card, see "Adding a Picture or Ringtone to a Contact" on page 83.

Viewing Pictures and Videos

Windows Phone includes some neat tricks to make browsing photos fun and easy. Remember that like just about everything else on your phone, photos respond to touch. And don't forget to try the semihidden filmstrip view, which lets you quickly flick through photos in an album.

View a Picture or a Video

(1) On Start, tap Pictures.

(2) Choose how you want to see your pictures organized— by album, date, or favorites.

(3) If necessary, tap an album to open it, and then tap the picture or video you want to view.

(4) If you tap a video, it starts playing. Use the playback controls to pause or resume it. If you tap a picture, you can:

- Flick left or right to see other pictures.

- Pinch a picture to its minimum size, then flick left or right to browse the album in filmstrip view.

- Spread your fingers to zoom in on an image.

- Double-tap a picture to instantly zoom out or in.

- Turn your phone sideways to view pictures in landscape view.

Tip ✓

In Date view, tap a heading to quickly jump to a different month or year.

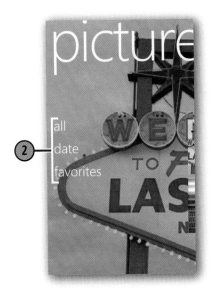

See Also

To learn how to display one of your photos on the lock screen, see "Changing Themes and Wallpaper" on page 26. To learn how to change the Pictures hub background, see "Personalizing the Pictures Hub" on page 198.

Tip

You can also see your videos in the Music + Videos hub. Tap Videos, and then flick to Personal.

Recording a Video

Pictures are great, but making your own movies is even more fun. Videos you take on your phone are deposited in the Camera Roll album and sport a tiny triangular Play icon. Alas, you have fewer options for sharing videos in Windows Phone 7 than you do with photos. You can't attach videos to text messages or e-mails or upload them to Facebook or Windows Live. At least not directly from your phone. However, new videos are automatically synched to your PC each time you connect (unless you specify otherwise).

Record a Video

1. Press the Camera button on your phone.

2. Tap to select video mode.

3. If necessary, tap Settings to adjust the video settings. (Options here vary by phone model.)

4. Tap the plus or minus sign to zoom in or out on your subject.

5. Press the Camera button to start recording your video. To stop recording, press it again.

6. When you're done, you can flick right to see how it turned out.

Tip ✔

Some Windows Phone 7 models can record high-definition (HD) video at 1280×720 pixel resolution. But to appreciate the HD recording, you have to watch it on a PC or TV with an HD screen. Video you play on the phone is always scaled down to 800×480 to fit the screen.

Saving Pictures to Your Phone

Not all the pictures you see in the Pictures hub are actually stored on your phone. Pictures from Facebook or Windows Live you see in What's New, for example, are stashed elsewhere on the Web. Ditto for photos attached to e-mails or texts. If you want to do anything with those images, you first have to save them to your phone. Once saved, the picture is automatically copied to your PC the next time you connect via the Zune software.

Save Pictures from Windows Live or Facebook

1. On the Start screen, tap Pictures.

2. Tap All.

3. Tap an online album, and then tap the picture you want to save to your phone.

4. Tap More.

5. Tap Save To Phone.

Tip

You can also save pictures from websites. In Internet Explorer, press and hold a picture, and then tap Save To Phone.

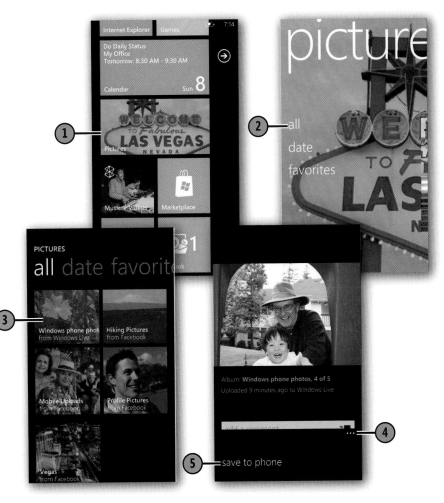

Saving Pictures to the Web

You can save (or *upload*) pictures you take on your phone to the Web, where they're easier to share. In Windows Phone 7 there are two possible destinations for your shots: Facebook or Windows Live SkyDrive, Microsoft's free online storage service. As you might expect, Microsoft has made SkyDrive an especially attractive destination. In fact, as long as you have an Internet connection, your phone can automatically save pictures you take to Windows Live, which can store up to 25 gigabytes' worth of shots. That makes SkyDrive a handy backup bin in case you accidentally lose your phone.

Upload a Picture

1. In the Pictures hub, find a photo you want to upload. (Sorry, no videos allowed.)

2. Tap More.

3. Tap Share.

4. Choose whether to upload your photo to Facebook or SkyDrive. If you want to add a caption, tap the caption text box, and then tap Upload. Otherwise, wait for Windows Phone to finish sending your photos.

See Also

To learn more about sending e-mail on your phone, see Section 7, "Reading and Sending E-Mail" starting on page 93. See Section 8, "Sending Text Messages," starting on page 109, to learn more about sending text messages on your phone.

Tip

You'll find photos uploaded to Facebook in Photos > My Uploads > Mobile Uploads on the Facebook site.

Turn On Automatic Uploading

① On Start, flick left to the Apps list, and then tap Settings.

② Flick to Applications, and then tap Pictures + Camera.

③ Tap to turn on Auto Upload to SkyDrive.

④ Choose a sharing permissions option.

⑤ Tap OK.

Caution

Photos you've taken before you turn on automatic uploading are not retroactively uploaded to Windows Live SkyDrive. Only photos you take after you turn on this feature are automatically saved there.

Tip

To see photos you've uploaded to Windows Live, visit photos.live.com and sign in with the Windows Live ID you've registered on your phone. Your photos are in the Mobile Photos folder.

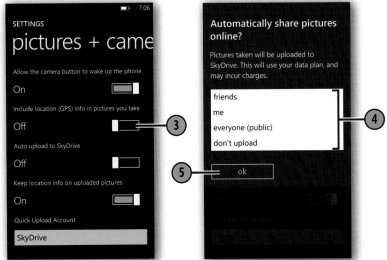

Synching Pictures and Videos to Your PC

By default, every picture or video you take on your phone is automatically copied (or *synched*) to your computer whenever you connect and open the Zune software. This is great for a couple of reasons. First, if you ever lose your phone or accidentally delete a photo or video from it, you're covered with a safety copy. Also, automated PC synching saves time if you plan to edit pictures or videos on your PC. If you don't want items to be automatically copied over, that's an option, too.

View Your Pictures

1. Connect your phone to your PC via the USB cable, and then open the Zune software.
2. Click Collection.
3. Click Pictures.
4. Click the album that matches the name of your phone.

View Your Videos

1. Connect your phone to your PC via the USB cable, and then open the Zune software.
2. Click Collection.
3. Click Videos.
4. Click Personal.

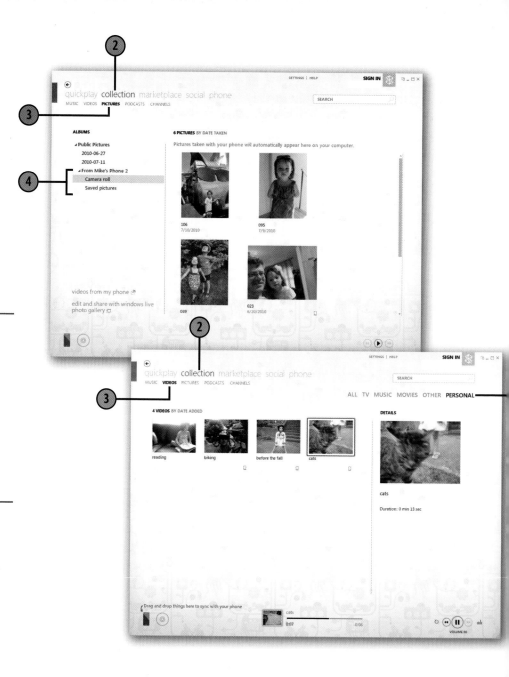

Change Sync Settings

1. Connect your phone to your PC via the USB cable, and then open the Zune software.

2. Click Settings.

3. Click Phone.

4. Click Pictures & Videos.

5. Under Import Settings, select the options you prefer.

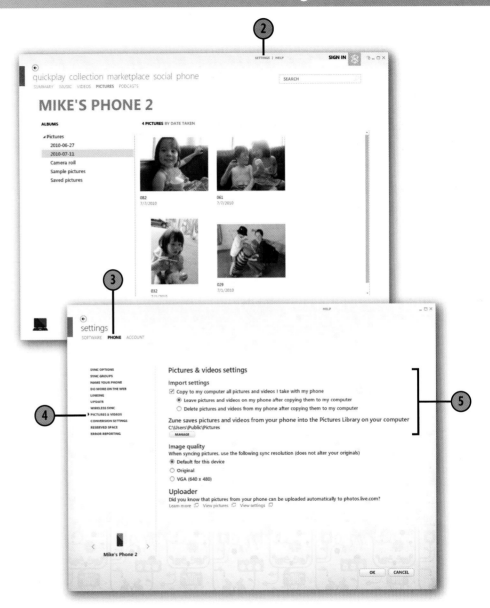

Creating a Favorites List

Once you start filling your phone with photos, it gets harder to quickly find the shots worth showing off to friends and family. That's where Favorites comes in. It's a place for the best of the best, so you don't have to waste time tapping and pecking around on your phone. Unfortunately, only photos can be promoted to your Favorites list. No videos allowed.

Add to Favorites

1. In the Pictures hub, browse to the photo you want to add to Favorites.

2. Tap More.

3. Tap Add To Favorites.

Tip

If you want to make a Facebook picture a favorite, you have to save it to your phone first. Press and hold the image, and then tap Save To Phone.

Tip

You can add a shortcut to Favorites on the Start screen by tapping and holding a picture in Favorites and then tapping Pin Favorites To Start.

Tip

To remove a photo from Favorites, tap More > Remove From Favorites.

Adding GPS Info to Pictures

Windows Phone comes with a built-in GPS receiver for showing your location on a map and getting directions. But GPS information can also be added to your pictures so that you know exactly where they were taken (or pretty close, at least). It gets better. Free photo-management programs such as Windows Live Photo Gallery and Google Picasa are designed to make use of this embedded GPS info—or *geotags*—to sort your collection by location or to show where a picture was taken on a map.

Add Location Info

1 On the Start screen, flick left to the Apps list or tap the arrow.

2 Tap Settings.

3 Flick to Applications, and then tap Pictures + Camera.

4 Tap to turn on Include Location (GPS) Info In Pictures You Take.

5 If you upload your photos to Facebook or Windows Live and don't want Windows Phone to automatically strip the geotags, turn on Keep Location Info On Uploaded Pictures.

Tip ✓

Why wouldn't you want to include geotags in images you post to Facebook and other public forums? Simple, your photo titled "Going to Hawaii for a Month!" could tip off a thief about where you live and how long you'll be gone. (Paranoid? Absolutely. But it's still possible.)

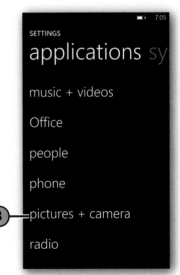

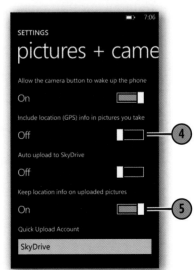

Personalizing the Pictures Hub

Few smartphones provide as many fun ways to showcase your photos. In addition to decorating the lock screen with your favorite snapshot, you can also personalize the Pictures hub background. Any picture you choose also shows up on the Start tile for the Pictures hub.

Change the Background

1. Tap and hold anywhere on the background in the Pictures hub.

2. Do one of the following:

   - Tap Change Background, and then select the picture you want to use as your background.

   - If you prefer to have your phone randomly choose a picture, tap Change It For Me.

See Also

To learn how to display a picture on the lock screen—another fun way to personalize your phone—see "Changing Themes and Wallpaper" on page 26.

Deleting Pictures and Videos

Pictures, and especially videos, can fill up your phone's onboard storage fast. If you need to make room for apps, music, or other goodies, you need to get rid of stuff you already have on your phone. Cleaning out the Pictures hub is easy; harder is deciding what to ditch. But if you've synched your phone with your PC using the Zune software, you should have copies on your computer of everything on your phone.

Delete a Picture or Video

1 In the Pictures hub, browse to the picture you want to delete.

2 Tap More.

3 Tap Delete.

Caution

This step only deletes a picture from your phone. If you've synched your photos to your PC using the Zune software (see Section 16 starting on page 239), you still have a copy in your Zune Pictures collection.

Delete an Album

1 In the Pictures hub, press and hold the album you want to delete.

2 Tap Delete.

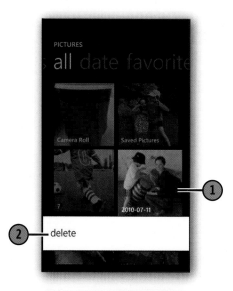

Clear the Camera Roll

1 In the Pictures hub, press and hold the Camera Roll.

2 Tap Clear.

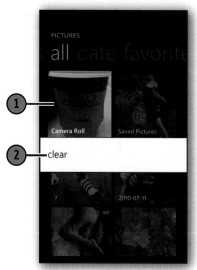

14 Shopping for Apps and Playing Games

Marketplace is Microsoft's virtual store for apps, games, music, TV shows, movies, podcasts—in other words, everything that makes your phone more fun and useful. In this section, you'll learn how to find and buy great apps and entertainment in Marketplace. I'll also cover the Games hub. With its strong Xbox pedigree, Windows Phone 7 is quickly shaping up to be a killer gaming machine.

You'll find Marketplace on both your phone and PC. Think of the PC version as the flagship store: It has everything Microsoft has to offer. The Marketplace hub on your phone is a branch outlet. It deals only in apps, games, and music. But the hub has the advantage of convenience, since you can shop directly on your phone. By the way, not everything in Marketplace costs money. Many apps and games are free. Some paid apps in Marketplace also let you try them before you buy them.

Speaking of games, Windows Phone is the first mobile device to fully weave in Xbox LIVE, Microsoft's hugely popular online gaming service, with more than 20 million subscribers. If you're one of them, you'll have access to your avatar, gamerscore, and other familiar Xbox goodies right on your phone. So let the fun begin!

Touring the Marketplace Hub

The Marketplace hub is one of the default tiles on your Start screen. The hub is divided into several areas, including a list of featured apps and a main menu. On the menu you can pick from Apps, Games, Music, or any custom category added by your cell-phone carrier. This screen also shows the status of items you're downloading and whether any software updates are available for apps already on your phone.

Apps—short for *applications*—are the add-on software programs that give smartphones their smarts. Because Windows Phone 7 is the new kid on the block, only time will tell how many you'll find for it in Marketplace. (As I write this, Marketplace isn't even open yet.) But early signs look promising. Marketplace is expected to have 16 categories of apps, including books, business, entertainment, finance, games, health and fitness, lifestyle, music and video, navigation, news and weather, photos, productivity, social, sports, tools, and travel.

The Marketplace hub is the place to get apps, games, and music for your phone

 Caution

You need a Windows Live ID to use Marketplace. If you don't already have a Windows Live ID, you'll be prompted to create or register one the first time you try to download an app.

Shopping for Apps and Games

Some apps and games in Marketplace are free. Others cost a few bucks. Depending on your carrier, you might have the option of rolling purchases onto your monthly phone bill. Otherwise, you can simply pay by credit card. To help you decide what to buy, each app should have a description and some screenshots. If other people have tried an app first, you might also find reviews.

Shop from Your Phone

1. On the Start screen, tap Marketplace.

2. In Marketplace, tap either Apps or Games on the main menu, depending on what you're looking for.

3. Flick to browse the subcategories and lists. When you find an app or game you like, tap it.

4. If an app or game is free, tap Install. Otherwise, do one of the following:

   • Tap Buy to pay for it. (You have to tap Buy again to confirm your choice.)

   • Tap Try to download a free trial version.

5. Apps you download or buy appear in the Apps list on your phone. Games show up under Collection in the Games hub.

Tip

If you don't want to put the cost of an app or a game on your phone bill, tap Change Payment Method when you check out. Then tap Add A Credit Card and follow the steps.

Caution

You need a Wi-Fi connection to download large apps and games on your phone. Only apps smaller than 20 megabytes can be downloaded via your cellular connection.

Shop from Your PC

① Connect your phone to your PC via the USB cable, open the Zune software on your computer, and then tap Marketplace.

② Click Apps.

③ Click Windows Phone.

④ Browse to find the app you want to try or buy, and then click it.

⑤ Click an available button—Try, Buy, or Free—and then follow any on-screen instructions.

Tip

If your phone is connected to your PC, the app is downloaded to your phone immediately. If you're phone isn't connected, the app is sent to your phone wirelessly within 24 hours.

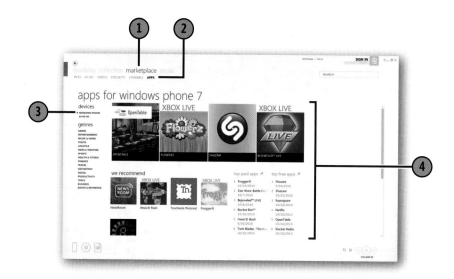

Searching Marketplace

There's so much stuff in Marketplace that you can quickly get bogged down by browsing. That's where your phone's Search button comes in. You can use the Search button to quickly pinpoint a specific app, game, song, album, artist, or playlist in Marketplace's vast collection. Obviously, the more specific you can be, the shorter the results list and less flicking you'll have to do.

Search on Your Phone

1. On the Start screen, tap Marketplace.

2. Press the Search button on your phone.

3. Tap the text box, and then type the term you're looking for.

4. Tap Go.

5. If you see the result you're looking for, tap it. Flick up and down to see more.

Tip

You can search three ways: by title, by keyword, or by the company that developed the item.

Shopping for TV Shows and Movies

Why would anybody watch a TV show or movie on a phone? I used to wonder the same thing—until I tried it. Turns out, it's a great way to kill time or entertain the kids when other options aren't available—on a bus, in an airport, or in a long line. TV shows and movies are available only on your PC. After you download one, you have to sync it to your phone. Marketplace sells popular TV shows and feature films. With movies, you also have the option to rent. Rentals are cheaper, but they have limitations: You have 14 days to start watching and 24 hours to finish a rental once you tap Play.

Buy a TV Show

① Connect your phone to your PC via the USB cable, open the Zune software, and then click Marketplace.

② Click Videos.

③ Click TV.

④ Browse to find the TV show you want to buy, and then click it.

⑤ Click Buy to purchase a single episode, or click Buy Season to purchase all episodes.

⑥ After the show is downloaded to your PC, browse to find it in your collection, and then drag it to the phone icon to sync it to your phone.

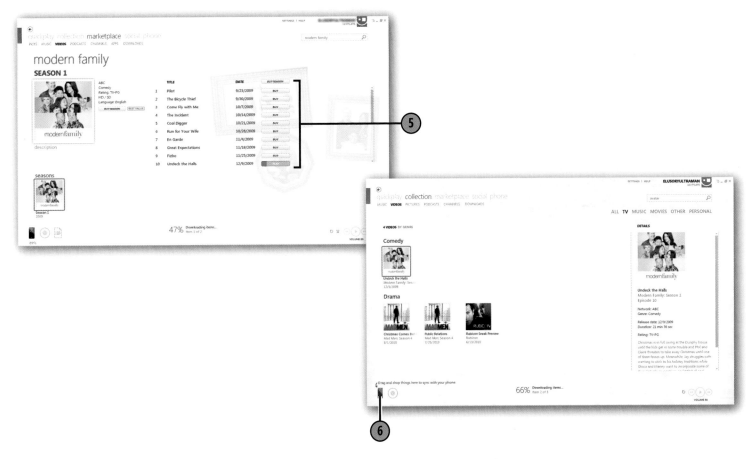

Buy or Rent a Movie

1 Connect your phone to your PC via the USB cable, open the Zune software, and then click Marketplace.

2 Click Videos.

3 Click Movies.

4 Browse to find the movie you want to buy or rent, and then click it.

5 Click Buy or Rent, and then follow the on-screen instructions to download the movie.

6 After the movie is downloaded to your PC, browse to find it in your collection, and then drag it to the phone icon to sync it to your phone.

Tip

Many Marketplace videos are available in both standard and high-definition versions. If you plan to watch them only on your phone, opt for the standard version to save money. Windows Phone can play high-def videos, but because the screen isn't HD, you won't notice much difference.

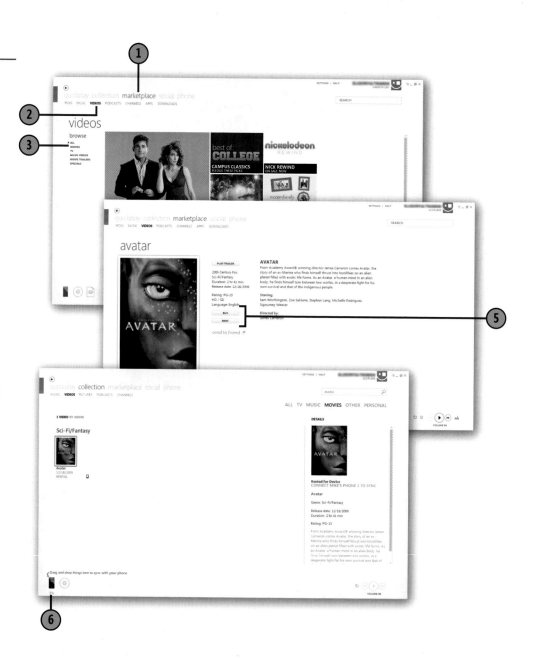

What's a Zune Pass?

Zune Pass is Microsoft's music subscription service. For a monthly fee—currently about $15—you can download or stream an unlimited amount of music from Marketplace directly to your phone or PC. Marketplace stocks millions of digital songs in MP3 format, so you shouldn't have trouble finding something you like. The music is protected by digital rights management (DRM) technology, which means that any music you download using your Zune Pass works only while you're a subscriber. Stop paying, and the music stops playing.

A Zune Pass is by no means the only subscription music service out there—others include Rhapsody, Napster, and Spotify, just to name a few. But Zune Pass is the only service specifically designed to work with Windows Phone. That alone makes it worth serious consideration.

Is a Zune Pass for you? It depends. If you're someone who loves music and enjoys sampling new artists and albums, then it's definitely worth a close look. A Zune Pass is also handy if you've left the house and forgotten to stock your phone with music, or if you hear a song you like and want to explore more from that artist. As a sweetener, Microsoft now allows you to download 10 songs a month for keeps. Factor that into the monthly subscription fee, and Zune Pass starts looking like a pretty sweet deal. Curious? Microsoft lets you try the service free for 14 days, so you can see whether it suits you. Visit *www. zune.net* to learn more.

Shopping for Music

If you have a Zune Pass subscription, you'll see options to download music from Marketplace directly to your phone. Subscribers can also stream music, which might be a good option if your phone storage is already getting full. If you don't have a Zune Pass, you have to pay for a song or an album to download it.

Buy or Download Music

(1) On the Start screen, tap Marketplace.

(2) Tap Music.

(3) Flick left or right to browse the categories: Features, New Releases, Top Albums, and Genres. Tap a genre such as rock or jazz to see even more choices.

(4) Tap the album you want to buy or listen to.

(5) If you have a Zune Pass subscription and want to stream a track or an album, just tap it. Otherwise, press and hold the album cover or a specific track, and then do either of the following:

- Tap Buy to purchase it.

- Tap Download to save it to your phone. (Requires a Zune Pass subscription.)

Tip

Any music you buy from Marketplace on your phone is automatically synched to your PC the next time you connect via the Zune software. That way, if you ever lose your phone, you still have what you paid for.

Tip

Marketplace isn't the only digital music store around. Amazon, Walmart, Apple, and other companies also sell music, which you can download to your PC and copy to your phone by using the Zune software. If the music isn't in a compatible format, the Zune software automatically converts it to a format that your phone can play.

Subscribing to Podcasts

You can download audio and video podcasts to your PC by using the Zune software and then connect your phone to sync them and take them with you. Marketplace has a solid lineup of podcasts to choose from, divided into 14 categories. You should have no problem finding something that interests you. The best part? They're all free.

Get Podcasts

1. Connect your phone to your PC via the USB cable, open the Zune software, and then click Marketplace.

2. Click Podcasts.

3. Browse to find the podcast you want to copy to your phone.

4. Do one of the following:

   - Click Subscribe to download three episodes.

   - Click Download to download individual episodes.

5. After a podcast is downloaded to your computer, browse to find it in your collection, and then drag it to the phone icon to copy it to your phone.

Uninstalling an App

If your phone starts to run short on storage, or if an app you downloaded isn't as cool as you thought it was going to be, you can easily delete it from your phone.

Uninstall an App

1 On the Start screen, flick left to the Apps list or tap the arrow.

2 Press and hold the app you want to remove from your phone.

3 Tap Uninstall. When you're asked for confirmation, tap Uninstall again.

Caution

Windows Phone 7 doesn't let you uninstall apps that come with the phone, like Alarm, Calculator, or Maps. You can uninstall only the apps you installed from Marketplace.

Tip

If you accidentally delete an app from your phone, you might not have to buy it again. Just find the item on Marketplace and tap Buy. On the confirmation screen, look for an option to reinstall the app or game.

Getting Around the Games Hub

Here's a fun fact: The majority of the smartphone apps made and sold today are games. Lots of people, it seems, are spending lots of time at play on their phones. The same will undoubtedly be true with Windows Phone 7, which is shaping up to be one heck of a portable game machine.

The Games hub is the place to play on your phone. The hub is divided into four areas: Collection, Spotlight, Xbox

LIVE, and Requests. Collection is where all your games are kept. Spotlight is a feed, providing game news and tips. The Xbox LIVE area is where members will find their gamer profile, including avatar, gamerscore, and achievements. (If these mean nothing to you, see "What's Xbox LIVE?" on page 217.) Finally, Requests is where you'll see invitations to play or reminders from opponents that it's your move.

News about new games, tips, and other offers

Turn on game requests

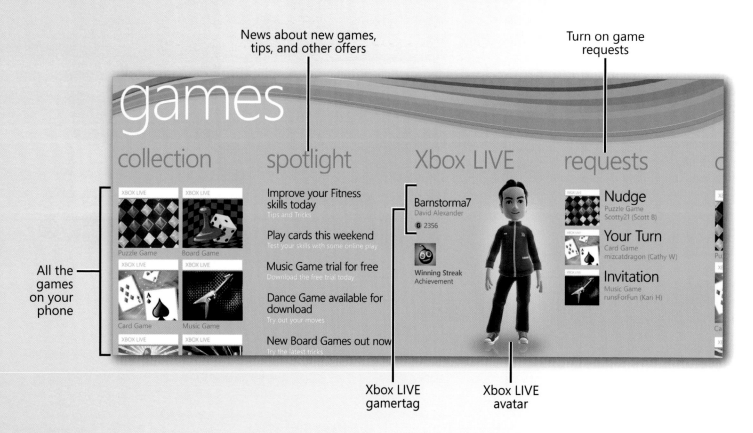

All the games on your phone

Xbox LIVE gamertag

Xbox LIVE avatar

Playing a Game

There are two ways to play on your phone. You can play solo or against other people. Games you download from Marketplace all show up in Collection within the Games hub. You won't find them in the Apps list.

Play a Game

1. On the Start screen, tap Games.

2. Flick to Collection.

3. Find the game you want to play, and then tap it.

Pin a favorite game to the Start screen. Press and hold the title you want to pin, and then tap Pin To Start.

Responding to Requests

Windows Phone 7 supports multiplayer games, so you can play against other people. Initially, the only kind of multiplayer game you'll be able to play on your phone is turn-based games. Microsoft has said there won't be any real-time multiplayer games, but that may change in the future. Until then, your friends can send you invitations to play and remind you that it's your move.

Answer a Game Request

① On the Start screen, tap Games.

② Flick left to Requests to see if a friend has invited you to play with them.

③ Tap the invitation to accept it and start playing.

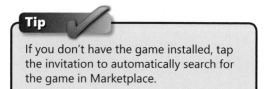

Tip

If you don't have the game installed, tap the invitation to automatically search for the game in Marketplace.

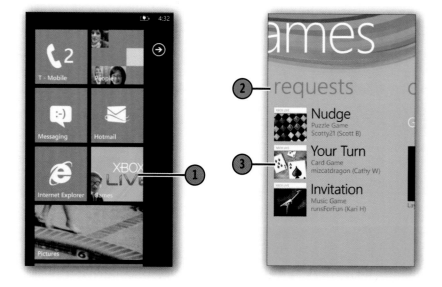

What's Xbox LIVE?

Xbox LIVE is Microsoft's online gaming and social networking service. First launched in 2002, the service started out as an extension of the company's popular Xbox gaming console. Later, Microsoft expanded the service to Windows PCs. Windows Phone 7 marks the first time it's been designed into a phone. The good news is that, unlike a Zune Pass, a basic Xbox LIVE subscription is free. And since the service already boasts more than 20 million subscribers, you shouldn't have any trouble finding someone to play against!

If you're new to video games, or grew up in the age of Pac-Man and Donkey Kong, the new online world of Xbox LIVE might feel a little foreign and intimidating at first. (I know it did for me.) But trust me: Once you familiarize yourself with a little of the Xbox LIVE lingo, you shouldn't have any problems having fun on your new smartphone. You'll probably also quickly discover that Xbox LIVE isn't just for hardcore gamers. Marketplace carries Xbox LIVE titles designed to appeal to a wide variety of ages, experience levels, and interests—from card games and word puzzles to cutting-edge shoot 'em ups.

Lingo of Xbox LIVE

If you're new to the world of Xbox or Xbox LIVE, it might help to learn a few of the basic concepts you'll run into:

- **Gamertag** Your gamertag is your unique user name on Xbox LIVE. You choose it when you sign up for an account.

- **Avatar** Avatars have become one of the hallmarks of Xbox. An avatar is your virtual self in the Xbox universe, your in-game alter ego. When you sign up for an Xbox LIVE account, you're asked to create an avatar, picking out its body type, facial features, hairstyle, clothes, and more. The fun of avatars is that they can be your mirror image or purely fantastical creations designed for fun.

- **Achievement points** Achievements are challenges within a game that you can complete to earn points. Achievements are totally optional, but they add another layer of excitement to a game. Achievement points can be earned for just about anything: finishing a particular level, killing a specific number of baddies, not dying, finding some object—anything!

- **Gamerscore** Your gamerscore is the total number of achievement points you've earned. A gamerscore is about bragging rights and also serves as a way to compare one player to another. (It's also a good indication of how game-addicted somebody is!)

Xbox LIVE Extras

Most of the basic game-related features of Xbox LIVE are available on Windows Phone 7. The Games hub, for example, shows your avatar, gamerscore, and achievements. But Microsoft has also created an add-on app called Xbox LIVE Extras that will let you have even more fun on your phone. Extras lets you dress and accessorize your avatar, see when your Xbox LIVE friends are online (and whether they're playing on their PC, Xbox console, or phone), send text messages to your Xbox LIVE friends, and see how your friends' achievements match up against yours. Look for Xbox LIVE Extras in Marketplace on your phone.

Setting Up an Xbox LIVE Account

You don't need an Xbox LIVE membership to play games on your phone, but having one makes Windows Phone 7 a lot more fun. If you don't already have an Xbox LIVE account, you can set one up right from your phone. There are two kinds of Xbox LIVE memberships: Silver and Gold. A Silver membership is free and lets you do most of the fun stuff you're probably itching to do on your phone.

Set up Xbox LIVE

① On the Start screen, tap Games.

② Flick to Xbox LIVE.

③ Do one of the following:

- If you've never used Xbox LIVE before, tap Join Xbox LIVE To Play With Friends, and follow the instructions.

- Otherwise, tap I Already Have An Xbox LIVE Account.

Uninstalling a Game

If your phone starts to run short on storage, or a game you downloaded isn't as cool as you thought it was going to be, you can easily delete it from your phone.

Uninstall a Game

1. On the Start screen, tap Games.

2. Flick to Collection.

3. Press and hold the game you want to delete.

4. Tap Uninstall. When you see the confirmation message, tap Yes.

15

Working with Office Mobile

Unlike Microsoft's previous line of smartphones, Windows Phone 7 is designed primarily for everyday life, not business. But I'm happy to report that it's still very work-friendly. As I've mentioned elsewhere, the phone fully supports Microsoft Exchange, which many companies use to power their employee e-mail and calendar systems.

Now let's focus on another of Windows Phone's business-friendly features: Office Mobile, which makes it easier to collaborate with coworkers and to get work done from the road. The Office hub comes with mobile versions of Word, Excel, PowerPoint, OneNote, and SharePoint Workspace. While it's possible to create some kinds of Office documents from scratch on your phone, Office Mobile is best for reviewing, editing, and commenting on existing files.

You probably know Word and PowerPoint, but this section covers a few Office apps that you might be less familiar with. SharePoint Workspace Mobile is handy if your company uses a Microsoft SharePoint site for storing and sharing documents. OneNote Mobile offers an easy way to make notes and lists on your phone, complete with pictures and voice memos. You can even sync OneNote notes to the Web so they're easier to share and study on your PC later.

Touring the Office Hub

The Office hub is divided into four sections. Two of these are devoted to SharePoint, Microsoft's popular technology for creating corporate intranet portals and document-sharing sites. If you don't use a SharePoint site at the office, you probably won't have much reason to venture to those parts of the hub. The other two areas are devoted to your OneNote notes and your documents. As you do with other hubs on the phone, you navigate from one area to another simply by flicking left or right with your finger. To open a document or note, just tap it.

The Documents area is where you'll find any Office document you create or save to your phone, including ones you receive as an e-mail attachment. The OneNote area is the repository for notes and lists you make. The main menu has only enough space for your six most recent notes. If you're an energetic list maker, that area will fill up fast. But a quick tap of the All icon will show you the complete catalog.

Tip

If you use Office frequently, you might want to pin it to the Start screen. On Start, flick to the Apps list, press and hold Office, and then tap Pin to Start.

Opening Documents

You can open any Office document on your phone, but you can create new documents only in Word or Excel. In many cases, Office documents look the same on your phone as they do on your PC, but you might occasionally see some differences because Office Mobile doesn't support the myriad formatting and style options available on the desktop. When you create or save an Office document to your phone, it shows up in the Office hub Documents list.

Open a Document

① On the Start screen, flick left to the Apps list or tap the arrow.

② Tap Office.

③ Flick to Documents.

④ Tap the Office document you want to open.

Like websites and maps, Office documents on your phone are also touch sensitive. Pinch your fingers on the screen to zoom out; spread them to zoom in on a document.

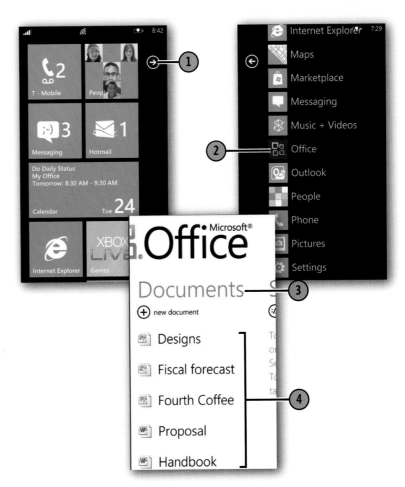

Create a New Document

1. In the Office hub, flick to Documents.

2. Tap New Document.

3. Tap the type of document you want to create.

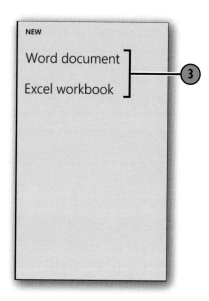

Sharing Documents via E-Mail

If you're editing or adding comments to a document on your phone, chances are you'll want to show it to someone at some point. You can send Office documents as e-mail attachments only from the Office hub.

Share a Document

(1) In the Office hub, flick to Documents, and then press and hold the document you want to share.

(2) Tap Send.

(3) Tap an e-mail account to use.

(4) Add the recipient and any other information to your message.

(5) Tap Send.

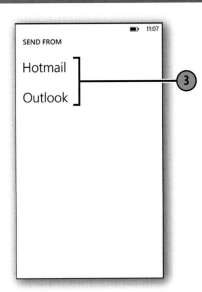

Saving and Deleting Documents

After you edit or make changes to a Word, Excel, or Power-Point document, you can save it to your phone as long as there's sufficient storage space. It's also just as easy to delete a document you no longer need.

Save a Document

1. When you finish editing an Office document, tap More.

2. Do one of the following:

   - Tap Save to save it with the current file name

   - Tap Save As to save the document with a new name. Type a new file name in the File Name box, and then tap Save.

See Also

To learn how to download an e-mail attachment to your phone, see "Working with Attachments" on page 102. If you receive a document as an e-mail attachment, you need to save it to your phone before you can start editing or adding comments to it.

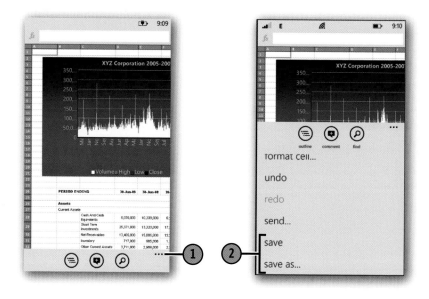

Delete a Document

1 In the Office hub, flick to Documents, and then press and hold the item that you want to delete.

2 Tap Delete. If you see a confirmation prompt, tap Yes to confirm.

Using Word Mobile

In Word Mobile, you can make tweaks to documents, change the formatting, or add comments. If a document contains section headers, you can also view it in Outline mode to quickly skip ahead to a section of interest.

Edit a Document

① In the Office hub, flick to Documents, and then tap a Word document.

② Tap Edit.

③ Do any of the following:

- Tap Format, and then choose the type of formatting to add. When you finish, repeat the process to turn off that formatting option.

- Tap Outline, and then tap the name of a section to go to that part of the document.

- Tap Find, type the word or number you want to locate, and then tap Enter.

- Tap Comment to add a note or remark to a document.

Tip

If you make a mistake, tap More > Undo. Tap Redo to reverse your mistake.

Using Excel Mobile

Excel Mobile on Windows Phone is a powerful tool. You can enter text and numbers in a work-sheet, change the worksheet's formatting, and much more.

Enter Numbers and Text

1 In the Office hub, open an Excel workbook.

2 Tap a cell.

3 Tap inside the formula bar, and type a number or text.

4 Tap Enter. Repeat as needed.

5 When you finish entering data, press the Back button to hide the keyboard.

> **Tip**
> To undo the last change you made, tap More > Undo. If you change your mind, tap Redo.

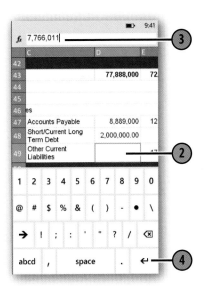

Switch Worksheets or Charts in a Workbook

① In an Excel workbook, tap Outline.

② Tap the worksheet or chart you want to see.

③ Press the Back button to exit.

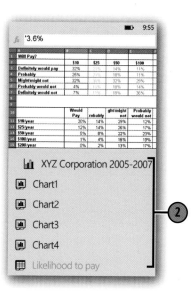

Add a Comment

① In an Excel workbook, tap the cell where you want to add a comment.

② Tap Comment.

③ Type your comment.

④ Tap outside the comment box to exit.

Tip

To delete a comment, tap the cell with the comment, and then tap More > Delete Comment.

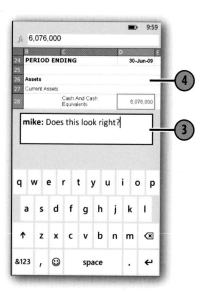

Using PowerPoint Mobile

Practice a PowerPoint presentation on the plane or in your hotel room. PowerPoint Mobile makes it easy to open and view slides, make small edits, and add notes.

Edit a Slide

(1) In the Office hub, open a PowerPoint presentation.

(2) Find the slide you want to change, and then tap Edit.

(3) Tap the selected text box or tap Edit.

(4) Edit the text as needed.

(5) Tap Done.

Add a Comment

1 In a PowerPoint presentation, tap the slide you want to comment on.

2 Tap Notes.

3 Type your comment.

4 Tap Done.

Tip

You'll see a small icon next to the slide number indicating there's a note. Tap Notes to read it. To edit a note, tap the text box, make your changes, and then tap Done.

Using OneNote Mobile

OneNote Mobile is a great general-purpose note taker, but you can also get creative and use your phone's camera or built-in microphone to record information for a note. For example, take a photo of a whiteboard during a meeting instead of transcribing the notes on it. Or dictate a quick voice memo before the idea slips away.

Create a New Note

 In the Office hub, flick to OneNote.

 Tap New Note.

 Tap the screen to compose your note. Add an optional title by tapping Enter Title.

 Optionally, you can also do one of the following:

- Tap List to insert a numbered list.

- Tap Picture to add a picture or take a new one with your camera.

- Tap Audio to add a voice or audio clip to a note.

 To save your note, press the Back or Start button.

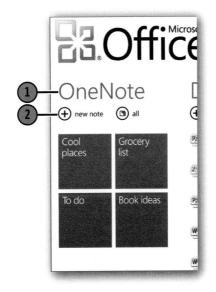

Tip
Your changes are saved automatically when you leave OneNote Mobile, so you won't lose what you've written if you have to take a call.

Tip
If you don't type a title, the first line of your note becomes the default title.

Tip
To create a bulleted list, tap More > Bulleted List.

Open a Saved Note

① In the Office hub, flick to OneNote.

② Tap the note to open it.

③ If you don't see the note you want, tap All, and then tap the note.

Tip

To delete a note, tap All, tap and hold the note you want to get rid of, and then tap Delete.

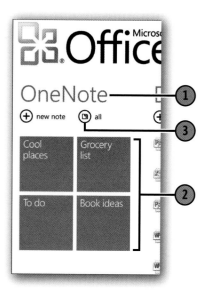

Synching Notes to the Web

If you have a Windows Live ID, you can use it to sync your OneNote notes to Windows Live on the Web. A notebook named Personal (Web) will be created on Windows Live and synched with your phone.

Set Up Sync

1 In the Office hub, flick to OneNote.

2 Tap All.

3 Tap Refresh. If prompted, tap Yes in the Sync With SkyDrive? message box.

Tip

To see your synched notes, log on to *www. windowslive.com*. In the main menu, click Office, click Recent Documents, and then click the OneNote file called Personal (Web). You can also access synched notes from *windowsphone. live.com*.

Caution

Changing the name of Personal (Web) might cause synching to stop working.

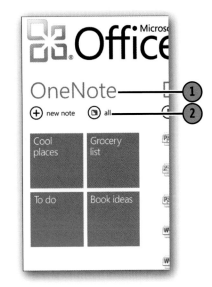

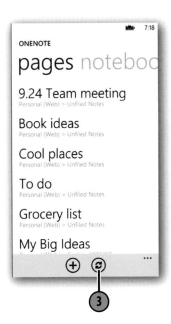

Open Synched Notes on Your Phone

1. In the Office hub, flick to OneNote.
2. Tap All.
3. Tap Refresh.
4. Tap Notebooks, tap a section under Personal (Web), and then tap the item you want to open.

Tip

Any changes you make are synched to your OneNote notebook on SkyDrive when you leave OneNote Mobile or tap Refresh.

Tip

To send a note as an e-mail attachment, open a note and tap Email. Enter the recipient and other info, and then tap Send.

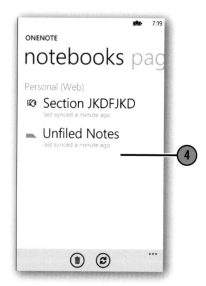

Connecting to SharePoint

SharePoint is a Microsoft technology that's used by a growing number of companies for employee websites, portals, intranets, blogs, wikis, and more. Windows Phone 7 is designed to work with Microsoft SharePoint 2010. On your phone, you can open Office documents stored on a SharePoint site, edit and make changes to them, and save them back to SharePoint for others to see.

Open a SharePoint Site

1. In the Office hub, flick to SharePoint.

2. Tap Open URL.

3. Next to http://, type the address for a SharePoint site, document library, list, or folder; and then tap Go. (If you see a sign-in prompt, enter your user name, password, and other credentials, and then tap Done.)

Tip

If you have an Exchange e-mail account set up on your phone, SharePoint tries to sign in using that user name and password.

Tip

Tap More > Bookmark This Link to add a tappable link to the SharePoint section of the Office hub.

Working with SharePoint Documents

You can open and edit Word documents, Excel workbooks, PowerPoint presentations, and OneNote notebooks from a SharePoint site on your phone. Make and save your changes as you normally would in the specific Office Mobile app, and the changes are saved back to the SharePoint site.

Edit and Save to SharePoint

1 In the Office hub, flick to SharePoint.

2 Tap All.

3 Flick to Links, and then tap a SharePoint site, document library, list, or folder.

4 Browse to the document you want to work on and tap it. A copy is downloaded to your phone.

Tip

Tap More > Bookmark This Link to add a link to a site, folder, or library to the SharePoint area of the hub.

Caution

To use SharePoint Workspace Mobile to access a SharePoint site inside your organization, you need to be connected to your company's network via Wi-Fi.

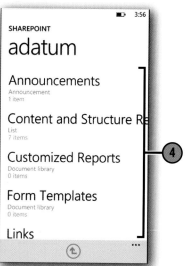

16 Synching with Your PC

If you're like most people, your PC has stuff on it, fun stuff you're probably itching to enjoy on your new Windows Phone—Bach or Beatles songs, TV episodes of *30 Rock*, podcasts from NPR, maybe even full-length movies. That's where synching comes in. Synching—short for synchronization—is the process of copying files back and forth between your PC and phone. Don't be put off by the nerdy-sounding name. Microsoft has made synching stuff to Windows Phone super easy. Most of the time it's drag, drop, and you're done.

The key is the free Zune software for your PC, which you are prompted to install the first time you connect your phone. (As this book went to press, Microsoft announced synching software for the Mac was also on the way.) Zune software is important to you for several reasons. First, you need it to receive software updates for your phone. The Zune software also features a more fully stocked version of Marketplace, with podcasts, TV shows, movies, and other goodies you can't get directly on the phone.

Synching isn't just about entertainment; it's also about safety. Every time you connect to your computer, the Zune software makes backup copies of pictures or videos you've shot with your phone. So if you ever lose it, your memories are safe.

Touring the Zune Software

As you've probably gathered, the Zune software is a key companion for your phone. It's a top-class media organizer and jukebox. It's a virtual store for music, TV shows, movies, and other digital entertainment. With its subtle animations and album-cover collages, it's also—let's just get this out there—drop-dead gorgeous.

While a complete explanation of the Zune software is beyond the scope of this book, let's take a quick look around. Provided your phone is connected to your PC, you'll see five main areas when you open the program. To navigate between them, use the menu at the top left.

Tip

To learn more about the Zune software's media organizing and playback abilities, visit *www.zune.net* and click Support > User's Guide > Zune Software.

Quickplay

Quickplay provides one-click access to favorite music, videos, or podcasts in your media collection. You'll see items you've recently added or played, and Quickplay is also the home of a feature called Smart DJ, which can whip up custom playlists based on your favorite album, artist, or song.

Collection

The heart of Zune, Collection is the library of music, pictures, videos, and podcasts on your PC (or at least the ones Zune knows about). Collection is also the place to sync songs and other media files to your phone.

Marketplace

Marketplace is Microsoft's entertainment store, the place to get music, TV shows, movies, podcasts, apps, games, and more. Some stuff is free. Other items you have to buy or rent. The Zune branch of Marketplace carries all the apps and entertainment Microsoft has to offer. You'll also find Marketplace on your phone, and while the Marketplace hub is more convenient, it carries only apps, games, and music.

Social

A social networking service that lets you find other people with similar musical tastes.

Phone

The latest addition to the Zune software, just for you and your Windows Phone. Here you can browse all the music, videos, pictures, and podcasts on your phone; find out how much storage space is left; and see a list of recently synched files.

Synching Media with Your Phone

The standard way to sync files to your phone is by dragging and dropping. But if your media collection is relatively small, you can also set up Zune so that everything on your PC is automatically copied over when you connect.

Sync Files

1. Open the Zune software on your PC, connect your phone using the USB cable, and then click Collection.

2. Click Music, Videos, Pictures, or Podcasts.

3. If necessary, click an option in the submenu to sort by artist, genre, album, or songs.

4. Click the item you want to sync.

5. While holding down the mouse button, drag the item to the phone icon. The item is copied to your phone.

Tip

Just about everything can be dragged and dropped in Zune: a song, an album, or a playlist. You can also drag and drop everything by an artist or an entire genre's worth of tunes.

Caution

You can't access certain features of your phone, such as the Pictures or Music + Videos hubs, while it's connected to your PC.

Tip

If you spot a small phone icon next to a song, video, picture, or other item in your collection, it means you've synched it to your phone already.

Seeing What's Synching

Once you start dragging and dropping, it's easy to lose track of what you've added to your phone. That's where the new Windows Phone summary screen comes in handy. It keeps a running account of every song, video, and podcast you copy from PC to phone and vice versa.

View Phone Status

1 Open the Zune software, connect your phone via the USB cable, and then click Phone.

2 Shows you what's currently synching with your phone. Click Stop Sync to prevent more files from being copied over.

3 Click Expand to see the inventory of files you've copied (or are currently copying) to or from your phone.

4 Shows how much space you've used up on your phone and how much remains. Hover your mouse over each section in the bar to see the breakdown by media type.

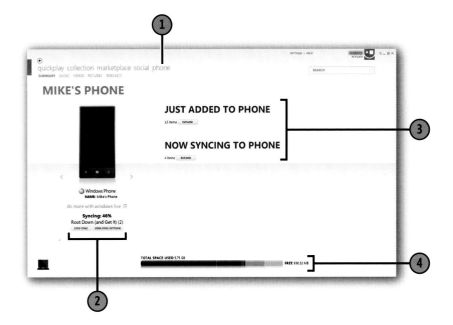

Tip

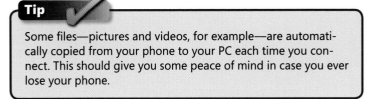

Some files—pictures and videos, for example—are automatically copied from your phone to your PC each time you connect. This should give you some peace of mind in case you ever lose your phone.

Synching Files Wirelessly

Here's a cool trick. If you have a Wi-Fi network at home, you can copy files from your PC to your phone over the airwaves. No USB cable required. Sound handy? It is. But there's a catch.

For wireless sync to work, your phone must be plugged into an AC power outlet. So technically, Microsoft hasn't cut all the wires yet.

Setup Wireless Sync

1 Open the Zune software, connect your phone via the USB cable, and then click Settings.

2 Click Phone.

3 Click Wireless Sync.

4 Click Set Up Wireless Sync.

5 Follow the on-screen instructions to complete the setup. Once setup is complete, just drag items to your phone as you normally would.

Caution

It might take up to 15 minutes for wireless synching to start working. There's no way to manually kick off the process. Also, synching won't occur if you're interacting with the phone or playing a song or video, for example. Finally, the phone must be plugged-in and charging.

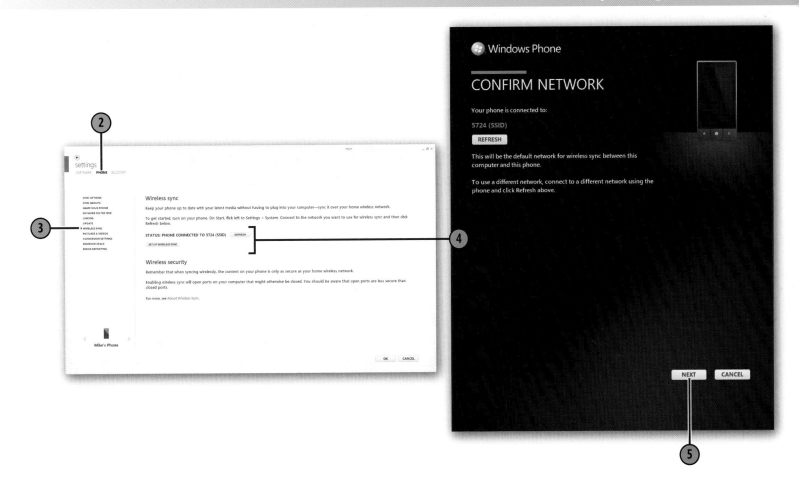

Adding Media to Your Zune Collection

Before you can sync music and videos to your phone, you have to stock your Zune collection. Put another way, if a song or video isn't in Zune, you can't copy it to your phone. If your PC is running Windows 7, Zune automatically scans your music, videos, pictures, and podcast libraries. But if you have stashed your media in other places—an external hard drive, for example—you have to tell Zune where it is.

Add Files

① Open the Zune software, and then click Settings.

② Click Software.

③ Click Collection.

④ Find the media type—music, pictures, videos, or podcasts—you want to add to your collection, and then click Manage.

⑤ Click Add, and then browse to find the folder that holds your media.

⑥ Click Include Folder. Zune scans the folder and adds its contents to your collection. Depending on the folder's size, a few minutes might pass before all the contents show up.

Tip

Do you have music in iTunes that you'd like to enjoy on Windows Phone? Just tell Zune where it is. As long as it's not copy-protected via digital rights management (DRM), you should be able to play it on your phone.

Tip

If you add music files to your Zune collection that Zune can't normally play, the software automatically converts them to a compatible format—handy if, say, you own an iPod or an iPhone and already have an extensive media library.

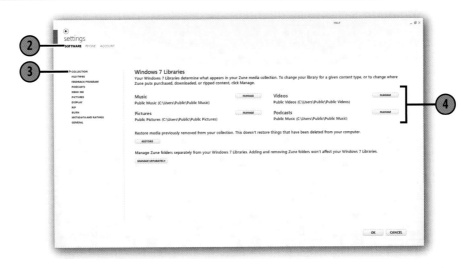

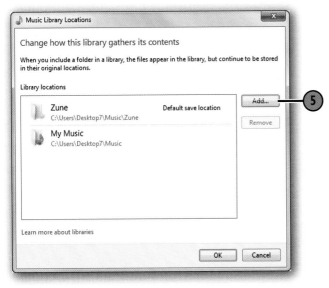

Changing Zune Sync Settings

Dragging and dropping is the default way to copy files onto your phone in Zune. But it doesn't have to be. You can tell Zune to sync everything on your PC to your phone. That way, any changes you make on your PC are automatically reflected on your phone (space permitting). You can also decide whether you want pictures and videos you take on your phone to be automatically copied to your computer each time you connect.

Change Music Settings

1. Open the Zune software, and then click Settings.

2. Click Phone.

3. Click Sync Options.

4. Under the media type you want to change, select one of the following:

   - Click All to sync everything to your phone.

   - Click Items I Choose if you want changes on your PC to be mirrored on your phone. (For example, delete something from your computer, and it's also gone from your phone.)

   - Click Manual if you don't want changes on your PC to be mirrored on your phone.

5. Select the Don't Sync Songs Rated check box if you want to keep songs you've rated unfavorably off your phone.

6. Click OK.

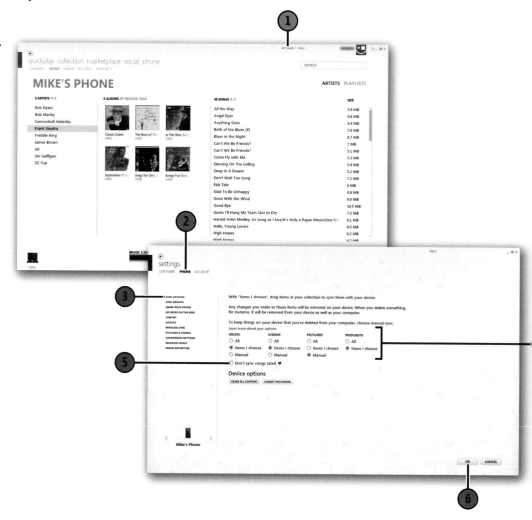

Change Picture and Video Settings

(1) Open the Zune software, and then click Settings.

(2) Click Phone.

(3) Click Pictures & Videos.

(4) Specify whether you want Zune to automatically copy pictures and videos on your phone to your PC, and whether you want them automatically erased andfrom your phone after a sync.

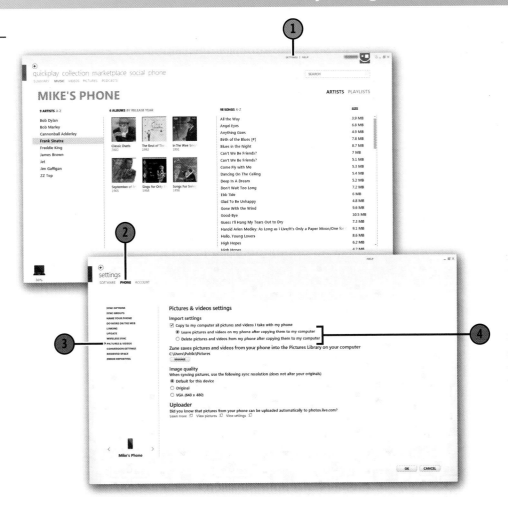

Managing Storage on Your Phone

Your phone's storage space can fill up fast, especially once you start snapping pictures and taking video. If you want to cram more onto your phone you can increase the amount of space reserved for e-mail and apps and pictures and videos you take. The downside? There's less space available from synching media files from your PC.

Adjust Space Settings

1 In the Zune software, click Settings.

2 Click Phone.

3 Click Reserved Space.

4 Drag the slider to the right to reserve more space for e-mail, pictures, and apps. If you prefer to sync more music and stuff from your PC, move the slider to the left instead.

5 Click OK.

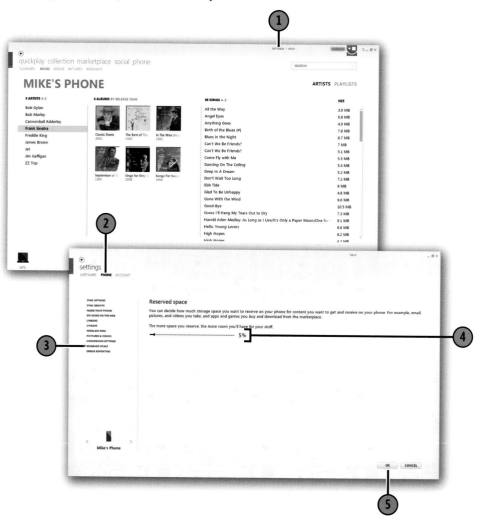

About the Author

Michael Stroh is a technology writer at Microsoft and has spent the last year working alongside the designers and engineers who created Windows Phone 7.

Before joining Microsoft in 2007, Michael spent more than a decade as a print journalist, most recently covering technology and science for the *Baltimore Sun*. His work has appeared in *Popular Science*, *ESPN Magazine*, the *Los Angeles Times*, and other publications.

Index

Symbols and Numbers

3G networks, 13
&123 keyboard key, 47
.com keyboard key, 45
+ (plus sign) icon, in Suggestion bar, 51

A

ABCD keyboard key, 47
About Card, calling up, 160
Accent Color option, 26
accepting/declining
    appointments, seeing status of, 122
    invitations, 130
accepting game requests, 216
achievement points in Xbox LIVE, 217
Add A Credit Card option in Marketplace, 203
Add An Account screen, 20–21
Add button
    for radio stations, 180
    for saving favorite websites, 145
Add Call tile, 65
Add contact button, choosing person from contact list, 111, 115
adding
    appointments, 122–123
    audio clips to notes, 233
    Bluetooth devices, 40–41

comments
    in documents, 228
    in Excel workbook, 230
    to PowerPoint presentation, 232
email accounts, 18
favorite websites, 145
files to folders on PC, 246
formatting to documents, 228
GPS info to pictures, 186, 197
Like/Unlike to comments, 86
map pushpins, 167
media to Zune Collection, 246
music tracks to Now Playing queue, 172
pictures to Favorites, 196
pictures to messages, 114–115
pictures to notes, 233
radio stations, 180
sender to contacts, 117
words to dictionary, 51
address bar, typing in Internet Explorer Mobile, 138
addresses
    finding contacts on maps using, 161
    importing, 32–33
    sharing, 164
    web suffixes, 138
Add To Favorites option, 196
Add To Now Playing option, 172
aerial views, map, 165
Agenda view in Calendar app
    about, 121
    changing, 126–127
    deleting appointments, 125
    proposing new appointment times, 131
    responding to invitations, 130
Airplane mode icon, 12
airplane mode, turning on/off, 39

Alarm set indicator, 9
albums, picture
    default, 186
    filmstrip view of, 188
albums, sharing music, 174
alerts, customizing, 28–29
alert sounds
    for appointment reminders, 124
    for new email messages, 96
All-day appointments, 123
Allow Cookies On My Phone option, 153
Allow The Camera Button To Wake Up The Phone feature, 187
Amazon music store, 211
Android phones, 5
Answer button, 63, 64
answering phone calls, 63
Apple music store, 211
appointments
    adding, 122–123
    changing calendar views for, 126–127
    deleting, 125
    editing, 124
    making private, 123
    notification of running late, 130
    on lock screen, 9
    proposing new times for, 131
    responding to, 130
    seeing details of, 120
    sending invitations for, 128–129
    showing attendees, 127
    viewing status of, 122
apps (applications)
    categories of, 202
    opening, with speech-recognition feature, 54
    pinning to Start screen, 7, 25
    reinstalling, 213

What do you think of this book?

We want to hear from you!

To participate in a brief online survey, please visit:

microsoft.com/learning/booksurvey

Tell us how well this book meets your needs—what works effectively, and what we can do better. Your feedback will help us continually improve our books and learning resources for you.

Thank you in advance for your input!

Stay in touch!

To subscribe to the *Microsoft Press® Book Connection Newsletter*—for news on upcoming books, events, and special offers—please visit:

microsoft.com/learning/books/newsletter